CAMBRIDGE
UNIVERSITY PRESS

Cambridge English

OFFICIAL

CAMBRIDGE PREPARATION MATERIAL

IELTS 12

ACADEMIC

WITH ANSWERS

AUTHENTIC EXAMINATION PAPERS

Cambridge University Press

www.cambridge.org/elt

Cambridge English Language Assessment

www.cambridgeenglish.org

Information on this title: www.cambridge.org/9781316637821

© Cambridge University Press and UCLES 2017

First published 2017

20 19 18 17 16 15 14 13 12 11 10 9 8 7 6 5 4 3 2 1

Printed in Malaysia by Vivar Printing

A catalogue record for this publication is available from the British Library

ISBN 978-1-316-63782-1 Academic Student's Book with answers
ISBN 978-1-316-63786-9 Academic Student's Book with answers with Audio
ISBN 978-1-316-63783-8 General Training Student's Book with answers
ISBN 978-1-316-63787-6 General Training Student's Book with answers with Audio
ISBN 978-1-316-63784-5 Audio CDs (2)

Contents

Introduction

The International English Language Testing System (IELTS) is widely recognised as a reliable means of assessing the language ability of candidates who need to study or work where English is the language of communication. These Practice Tests are designed to give future IELTS candidates an idea of whether their English is at the required level.

IELTS is owned by three partners, Cambridge English Language Assessment, part of the University of Cambridge, the British Council and IDP Education Pty Limited (through its subsidiary company, IELTS Australia Pty Limited). Further information on IELTS can be found on the IELTS website www.ielts.org.

WHAT IS THE TEST FORMAT?

IELTS consists of four components. All candidates take the same Listening and Speaking tests. There is a choice of Reading and Writing tests according to whether a candidate is taking the Academic or General Training module.

Academic	General Training
For candidates wishing to study at undergraduate or postgraduate levels, and for those seeking professional registration.	For candidates wishing to migrate to an English-speaking country (Australia, Canada, New Zealand, UK), and for those wishing to train or study at below degree level.

The test components are taken in the following order:

Listening		
4 sections, 40 items, approximately 30 minutes		
Academic Reading 3 sections, 40 items 60 minutes	or	**General Training Reading** 3 sections, 40 items 60 minutes
Academic Writing 2 tasks 60 minutes	or	**General Training Writing** 2 tasks 60 minutes
Speaking 11 to 14 minutes		
Total Test Time 2 hours 44 minutes		

ACADEMIC TEST FORMAT

Listening

This test consists of four sections, each with ten questions. The first two sections are concerned with social needs. The first section is a conversation between two speakers and the second section is a monologue. The final two sections are concerned with situations related to educational or training contexts. The third section is a conversation between up to four people and the fourth section is a monologue.

A variety of question types is used, including: multiple choice, matching, plan/map/ diagram labelling, form completion, note completion, table completion, flow-chart completion, summary completion, sentence completion and short-answer questions.

Candidates hear the recording once only and answer the questions as they listen. Ten minutes are allowed at the end for candidates to transfer their answers to the answer sheet.

Reading

This test consists of three sections with 40 questions. There are three texts, which are taken from journals, books, magazines and newspapers. The texts are on topics of general interest. At least one text contains detailed logical argument.

A variety of question types is used, including: multiple choice, identifying information (True/False/Not Given), identifying the writer's views/claims (Yes/No/Not Given), matching information, matching headings, matching features, matching sentence endings, sentence completion, summary completion, note completion, table completion, flow-chart completion, diagram label completion and short-answer questions.

Writing

This test consists of two tasks. It is suggested that candidates spend about 20 minutes on Task 1, which requires them to write at least 150 words, and 40 minutes on Task 2, which requires them to write at least 250 words. Task 2 contributes twice as much as Task 1 to the Writing score.

Task 1 requires candidates to look at a diagram or some data (in a graph, table or chart) and to present the information in their own words. They are assessed on their ability to organise, present and possibly compare data, and are required to describe the stages of a process, describe an object or event, or explain how something works.

In Task 2, candidates are presented with a point of view, argument or problem. They are assessed on their ability to present a solution to the problem, present and justify an opinion, compare and contrast evidence and opinions, and to evaluate and challenge ideas, evidence or arguments.

Candidates are also assessed on their ability to write in an appropriate style. More information on assessing the Writing test, including Writing assessment criteria (public version), is available on the IELTS website.

Speaking

This test takes between 11 and 14 minutes and is conducted by a trained examiner. There are three parts:

Part 1

The candidate and the examiner introduce themselves. Candidates then answer general questions about themselves, their home/family, their job/studies, their interests and a wide range of similar familiar topic areas. This part lasts between four and five minutes.

Part 2

The candidate is given a task card with prompts and is asked to talk on a particular topic. The candidate has one minute to prepare and they can make some notes if they wish, before speaking for between one and two minutes. The examiner then asks one or two questions on the same topic.

Part 3

The examiner and the candidate engage in a discussion of more abstract issues which are thematically linked to the topic in Part 2. The discussion lasts between four and five minutes.

The Speaking test assesses whether candidates can communicate effectively in English. The assessment takes into account Fluency and Coherence, Lexical Resource, Grammatical Range and Accuracy, and Pronunciation. More information on assessing the Speaking test, including Speaking assessment criteria (public version), is available on the IELTS website.

HOW IS IELTS SCORED?

IELTS results are reported on a nine-band scale. In addition to the score for overall language ability, IELTS provides a score in the form of a profile for each of the four skills (Listening, Reading, Writing and Speaking). These scores are also reported on a nine-band scale. All scores are recorded on the Test Report Form along with details of the candidate's nationality, first language and date of birth. Each Overall Band Score corresponds to a descriptive statement which gives a summary of the English language ability of a candidate classified at that level. The nine bands and their descriptive statements are as follows:

9 **Expert User** – *Has fully operational command of the language: appropriate, accurate and fluent with complete understanding.*

8 **Very Good User** – *Has fully operational command of the language with only occasional unsystematic inaccuracies and inappropriacies. Misunderstandings may occur in unfamiliar situations. Handles complex detailed argumentation well.*

7 **Good User** – *Has operational command of the language, though with occasional inaccuracies, inappropriacies and misunderstandings in some situations. Generally handles complex language well and understands detailed reasoning.*

6 **Competent User** – *Has generally effective command of the language despite some inaccuracies, inappropriacies and misunderstandings. Can use and understand fairly complex language, particularly in familiar situations.*

5 **Modest User** – *Has partial command of the language, coping with overall meaning in most situations, though is likely to make many mistakes. Should be able to handle basic communication in own field.*

4 **Limited User** – *Basic competence is limited to familiar situations. Has frequent problems in understanding and expression. Is not able to use complex language.*

3 **Extremely Limited User** – *Conveys and understands only general meaning in very familiar situations. Frequent breakdowns in communication occur.*

2 **Intermittent User** – *No real communication is possible except for the most basic information using isolated words or short formulae in familiar situations and to meet immediate needs. Has great difficulty understanding spoken and written English.*

1 **Non User** – *Essentially has no ability to use the language beyond possibly a few isolated words.*

0 **Did not attempt the test** – *No assessable information provided.*

MARKING THE PRACTICE TESTS

Listening and Reading

The Answer Keys are on pages 116–123.
Each question in the Listening and Reading tests is worth one mark.

Questions which require letter / Roman numeral answers

- For questions where the answers are letters or Roman numerals, you should write *only* the number of answers required. For example, if the answer is a single letter or numeral you should write only one answer. If you have written more letters or numerals than are required, the answer must be marked wrong.

Questions which require answers in the form of words or numbers

- Answers may be written in upper or lower case.
- Words in brackets are *optional* – they are correct, but not necessary.
- Alternative answers are separated by a slash (/).
- If you are asked to write an answer using a certain number of words and/or (a) number(s), you will be penalised if you exceed this. For example, if a question specifies an answer using NO MORE THAN THREE WORDS and the correct answer is 'black leather coat', the answer 'coat of black leather' is *incorrect*.
- In questions where you are expected to complete a gap, you should only transfer the necessary missing word(s) onto the answer sheet. For example, to complete 'in the …', where the correct answer is 'morning', the answer 'in the morning' would be *incorrect*.
- All answers require correct spelling (including words in brackets).
- Both US and UK spelling are acceptable and are included in the Answer Key.
- All standard alternatives for numbers, dates and currencies are acceptable.
- All standard abbreviations are acceptable.
- You will find additional notes about individual answers in the Answer Key.

Writing

The sample answers are on pages 124–131. It is not possible for you to give yourself a mark for the Writing tasks. We have provided sample answers (written by candidates), showing their score and the examiner's comments. These sample answers will give you an insight into what is required for the Writing test.

HOW SHOULD YOU INTERPRET YOUR SCORES?

At the end of each Listening and Reading Answer Key you will find a chart which will help you assess whether, on the basis of your Practice Test results, you are ready to take the IELTS test.

In interpreting your score, there are a number of points you should bear in mind. Your performance in the real IELTS test will be reported in two ways: there will be a Band Score from 1 to 9 for each of the components and an Overall Band Score from 1 to 9, which is the average of your scores in the four components. However, institutions considering your application are advised to look at both the Overall Band Score and the Bands for each component in order to determine whether you have the language skills needed for a particular course of study. For example, if your course involves a lot of reading and writing, but no lectures, listening skills might be less important and a score of 5 in Listening might be acceptable if the Overall Band Score was 7. However, for a course which has lots of lectures and spoken instructions, a score of 5 in Listening might be unacceptable even though the Overall Band Score was 7.

Once you have marked your tests, you should have some idea of whether your listening and reading skills are good enough for you to try the IELTS test. If you did well enough in one component, but not in others, you will have to decide for yourself whether you are ready to take the test.

The Practice Tests have been checked to ensure that they are of approximately the same level of difficulty as the real IELTS test. However, we cannot guarantee that your score in the Practice Tests will be reflected in the real IELTS test. The Practice Tests can only give you an idea of your possible future performance and it is ultimately up to you to make decisions based on your score.

Different institutions accept different IELTS scores for different types of courses. We have based our recommendations on the average scores which the majority of institutions accept. The institution to which you are applying may, of course, require a higher or lower score than most other institutions.

Further information

For more information about IELTS or any other Cambridge English Language Assessment examination, write to:

Cambridge English Language Assessment
1 Hills Road
Cambridge
CB1 2EU
United Kingdom

https://support.cambridgeenglish.org
http://www.ielts.org

Test 5

SECTION 1   *Questions 1–10*

Complete the notes below.

*Write **ONE WORD AND/OR A NUMBER** for each answer.*

FAMILY EXCURSIONS

Cruise on a lake

Example

- Travel on an old ....*steamship*.........

- Can take photos of the **1** .... that surround the lake

Farm visit

- Children can help feed the sheep
- Visit can include a 40-minute ride on a **2** ....
- Visitors can walk in the farm's **3** .... by the lake
- **4** .... is available at extra cost

Cycling trips

- Cyclists explore the Back Road
- A **5** .... is provided
- Only suitable for cyclists who have some **6** ....
    - Bikes can be hired from **7** .... (near the Cruise Ship Terminal)

10

- Cyclists need:
    - a repair kit
    - food and drink
    - a **8** .... (can be hired)
- There are no **9** .... or accommodation in the area

Cost

- Total cost for whole family of cruise and farm visit: **10** $ ....

SECTION 2   *Questions 11–20*

Questions 11–14

*Choose the correct letter, **A**, **B** or **C**.*

Talk to new kitchen assistants

11 According to the manager, what do most people like about the job of kitchen assistant?

    A   the variety of work
    B   the friendly atmosphere
    C   the opportunities for promotion

12 The manager is concerned about some of the new staff's

    A   jewellery.
    B   hair styles.
    C   shoes.

13 The manager says that the day is likely to be busy for kitchen staff because

    A   it is a public holiday.
    B   the head chef is absent.
    C   the restaurant is almost fully booked.

14 Only kitchen staff who are 18 or older are allowed to use

    A   the waste disposal unit.
    B   the electric mixer.
    C   the meat slicer.

Questions 15 and 16

*Choose **TWO** letters, **A–E**.*

According to the manager, which **TWO** things can make the job of kitchen assistant stressful?

    A   They have to follow orders immediately.
    B   The kitchen gets very hot.
    C   They may not be able to take a break.
    D   They have to do overtime.
    E   The work is physically demanding.

Questions 17–20

What is the responsibility of each of the following restaurant staff?

*Choose **FOUR** answers from the box and write the correct letter, **A–F**, next to Questions 17–20.*

Responsibilities
A   training courses
B   food stocks
C   first aid
D   breakages
E   staff discounts
F   timetables

Restaurant staff

17   Joy Parkins   ....

18   David Field   ....

19   Dexter Wills   ....

20   Mike Smith   ....

SECTION 3   *Questions 21–30*

Questions 21–23

*Choose the correct letter, **A**, **B** or **C**.*

Paper on Public Libraries

21 What will be the main topic of Trudie and Stewart's paper?

  A   how public library services are organised in different countries
  B   how changes in society are reflected in public libraries
  C   how the funding of public libraries has changed

22 They agree that one disadvantage of free digitalised books is that

  A   they may take a long time to read.
  B   they can be difficult to read.
  C   they are generally old.

23 Stewart expects that in the future libraries will

  A   maintain their traditional function.
  B   become centres for local communities.
  C   no longer contain any books.

Questions 24–30

Complete the notes below.

*Write **ONE WORD ONLY** for each answer.*

Study of local library: possible questions

• whether it has a **24** .... of its own

• its policy regarding noise of various kinds

• how it's affected by laws regarding all aspects of **25** ....

• how the design needs to take the **26** .... of customers into account

• what **27** .... is required in case of accidents

• why a famous person's **28** .... is located in the library

• whether it has a **29** .... of local organisations

• how it's different from a library in a **30** ....

SECTION 4   *Questions 31–40*

Complete the notes below.

*Write **NO MORE THAN TWO WORDS** for each answer.*

Four business values

Many business values can result in **31** ....

Senior managers need to understand and deal with the potential
32 .... that may result.

Collaboration

During a training course, the speaker was in a team that had to build a
33 ....

Other teams experienced **34** .... from trying to collaborate.

The speaker's team won because they reduced collaboration.

Sales of a **35** .... were poor because of collaboration.

Industriousness

Hard work may be a bad use of various company **36** ....

The word 'lazy' in this context refers to people who avoid doing tasks that
are **37** ....

Creativity

An advertising campaign for a **38** .... was memorable but failed to
boost sales.

Creativity should be used as a response to a particular **39** ....

Excellence

According to one study, on average, pioneers had a **40** .... that
was far higher than that of followers.

Companies that always aim at excellence may miss opportunities.

READING

READING PASSAGE 1

*You should spend about 20 minutes on **Questions 1–13**, which are based on Reading Passage 1 below.*

Cork

Cork – the thick bark of the cork oak tree (*Quercus suber)* – is a remarkable material. It is tough, elastic, buoyant, and fire-resistant, and suitable for a wide range of purposes. It has also been used for millennia: the ancient Egyptians sealed their sarcophagi (stone coffins) with cork, while the ancient Greeks and Romans used it for anything from beehives to sandals.

And the cork oak itself is an extraordinary tree. Its bark grows up to 20 cm in thickness, insulating the tree like a coat wrapped around the trunk and branches and keeping the inside at a constant 20°C all year round. Developed most probably as a defence against forest fires, the bark of the cork oak has a particular cellular structure – with about 40 million cells per cubic centimetre – that technology has never succeeded in replicating. The cells are filled with air, which is why cork is so buoyant. It also has an elasticity that means you can squash it and watch it spring back to its original size and shape when you release the pressure.

Cork oaks grow in a number of Mediterranean countries, including Portugal, Spain, Italy, Greece and Morocco. They flourish in warm, sunny climates where there is a minimum of 400 millimetres of rain per year, and not more than 800 millimetres. Like grape vines, the trees thrive in poor soil, putting down deep roots in search of moisture and nutrients. Southern Portugal's Alentejo region meets all of these requirements, which explains why, by the early 20th century, this region had become the world's largest producer of cork, and why today it accounts for roughly half of all cork production around the world.

Most cork forests are family-owned. Many of these family businesses, and indeed many of the trees themselves, are around 200 years old. Cork production is, above all, an exercise in patience. From the planting of a cork sapling to the first harvest takes 25 years, and a gap of approximately a decade must separate harvests from an individual tree. And for top-quality cork, it's necessary to wait a further 15 or 20 years. You even have to wait for the right kind of summer's day to harvest cork. If the bark is stripped on a day when it's too cold – or when the air is damp – the tree will be damaged.

Cork harvesting is a very specialised profession. No mechanical means of stripping cork bark has been invented, so the job is done by teams of highly skilled workers. First, they make vertical cuts down the bark using small sharp axes, then lever it away in pieces as large as they can manage. The most skilful cork-strippers prise away a semi-circular husk that runs the length of the trunk from just above ground level to the first branches. It is then dried on the ground for about four months, before being taken to factories, where it is boiled to kill any insects that might remain in the cork. Over 60% of cork then goes on to be made into traditional bottle stoppers, with most of the remainder being used in the construction trade. Corkboard and cork tiles are ideal for thermal and acoustic insulation, while granules of cork are used in the manufacture of concrete.

Recent years have seen the end of the virtual monopoly of cork as the material for bottle stoppers, due to concerns about the effect it may have on the contents of the bottle. This is caused by a chemical compound called 2,4,6-trichloroanisole (TCA), which forms through the interaction of plant phenols, chlorine and mould. The tiniest concentrations – as little as three or four parts to a trillion – can spoil the taste of the product contained in the bottle. The result has been a gradual yet steady move first towards plastic stoppers and, more recently, to aluminium screw caps. These substitutes are cheaper to manufacture and, in the case of screw caps, more convenient for the user.

The classic cork stopper does have several advantages, however. Firstly, its traditional image is more in keeping with that of the type of high quality goods with which it has long been associated. Secondly – and very importantly – cork is a sustainable product that can be recycled without difficulty. Moreover, cork forests are a resource which support local biodiversity, and prevent desertification in the regions where they are planted. So, given the current concerns about environmental issues, the future of this ancient material once again looks promising.

Questions 1–5

Do the following statements agree with the information given in Reading Passage 1?

In boxes 1–5 on your answer sheet, write

> **TRUE**   *if the statement agrees with the information*
> **FALSE**   *if the statement contradicts the information*
> **NOT GIVEN** *if there is no information on this*

1   The cork oak has the thickest bark of any living tree.

2   Scientists have developed a synthetic cork with the same cellular structure as natural cork.

3   Individual cork oak trees must be left for 25 years between the first and second harvest.

4   Cork bark should be stripped in dry atmospheric conditions.

5   The only way to remove the bark from cork oak trees is by hand.

Questions 6–13

Complete the notes below.

Choose ONE WORD ONLY from the passage for each answer.

Write your answers in boxes 6–13 on your answer sheet.

Comparison of aluminium screw caps and cork bottle stoppers

Advantages of aluminium screw caps

- do not affect the **6** .... of the bottle contents
- are **7** .... to produce
- are **8** .... to use

Advantages of cork bottle stoppers

- suit the **9** .... of quality products
- made from a **10** .... material
- easily **11** ....
- cork forests aid **12** ....
- cork forests stop **13** .... happening

READING PASSAGE 2

*You should spend about 20 minutes on **Questions 14–26**, which are based on Reading Passage 2 below.*

COLLECTING AS A HOBBY

Collecting must be one of the most varied of human activities, and it's one that many of us psychologists find fascinating. Many forms of collecting have been dignified with a technical name: an archtophilist collects teddy bears, a philatelist collects postage stamps, and a deltiologist collects postcards. Amassing hundreds or even thousands of postcards, chocolate wrappers or whatever, takes time, energy and money that could surely be put to much more productive use. And yet there are millions of collectors around the world. Why do they do it?

There are the people who collect because they want to make money – this could be called an instrumental reason for collecting; that is, collecting as a means to an end. They'll look for, say, antiques that they can buy cheaply and expect to be able to sell at a profit. But there may well be a psychological element, too – buying cheap and selling dear can give the collector a sense of triumph. And as selling online is so easy, more and more people are joining in.

Many collectors collect to develop their social life, attending meetings of a group of collectors and exchanging information on items. This is a variant on joining a bridge club or a gym, and similarly brings them into contact with like-minded people.

Another motive for collecting is the desire to find something special, or a particular example of the collected item, such as a rare early recording by a particular singer.

Some may spend their whole lives in a hunt for this. Psychologically, this can give a purpose to a life that otherwise feels aimless. There is a danger, though, that if the individual is ever lucky enough to find what they're looking for, rather than celebrating their success, they may feel empty, now that the goal that drove them on has gone.

If you think about collecting postage stamps, another potential reason for it – or, perhaps, a result of collecting – is its educational value. Stamp collecting opens a window to other countries, and to the plants, animals, or famous people shown on their stamps. Similarly, in the 19th century, many collectors amassed fossils, animals and plants from around the globe, and their collections provided a vast amount of information about the natural world. Without those collections, our understanding would be greatly inferior to what it is.

In the past – and nowadays, too, though to a lesser extent – a popular form of collecting, particularly among boys and men, was trainspotting. This might involve trying to see every locomotive of a particular type, using published data that identifies each one, and ticking off each engine as it is seen. Trainspotters exchange information, these days often by mobile phone, so they can work out where to go to, to see a particular engine. As a by-product, many practitioners of the hobby become very knowledgeable about railway operations, or the technical specifications of different engine types.

Similarly, people who collect dolls may go beyond simply enlarging their collection, and develop an interest in the way that dolls are made, or the materials that are used. These have changed over the centuries from the wood that was standard in 16th century Europe, through the wax and porcelain of later centuries, to the plastics of today's dolls. Or collectors might be inspired to study how dolls reflect notions of what children like, or ought to like.

Not all collectors are interested in learning from their hobby, though, so what we might call a psychological reason for collecting is the need for a sense of control, perhaps as a way of dealing with insecurity. Stamp collectors, for instance, arrange their stamps in albums, usually very neatly, organising their collection according to certain commonplace principles –

perhaps by country in alphabetical order, or grouping stamps by what they depict – people, birds, maps, and so on.

One reason, conscious or not, for *what* someone chooses to collect is to show the collector's individualism. Someone who decides to collect something as unexpected as dog collars, for instance, may be conveying their belief that they must be interesting themselves. And believe it or not, there is at least one dog collar museum in existence, and it grew out of a personal collection.

Of course, all hobbies give pleasure, but the common factor in collecting is usually passion: pleasure is putting it far too mildly. More than most other hobbies, collecting can be totally engrossing, and can give a strong sense of personal fulfilment. To non-collectors it may appear an eccentric, if harmless, way of spending time, but potentially, collecting has a lot going for it.

Questions 14–21

Complete the sentences below.

*Choose **ONE WORD ONLY** from the passage for each answer.*

Write your answers in boxes 14–21 on your answer sheet.

14 The writer mentions collecting ………… as an example of collecting in order to make money.

15 Collectors may get a feeling of ………… from buying and selling items.

16 Collectors' clubs provide opportunities to share ………… .

17 Collectors' clubs offer ………… with people who have similar interests.

18 Collecting sometimes involves a life-long ………… for a special item.

19 Searching for something particular may prevent people from feeling their life is completely ………… .

20 Stamp collecting may be ………… because it provides facts about different countries.

21 ………… tends to be mostly a male hobby.

Questions 22–26

Do the following statements agree with the information given in the passage on *pages 20 and 21?*

In boxes 22–26 on your answer sheet, write

> **TRUE**   *if the statement agrees with the information*
> **FALSE**   *if the statement contradicts the information*
> **NOT GIVEN** *if there is no information on this*

22 The number of people buying dolls has grown over the centuries.

23 Sixteenth century European dolls were normally made of wax and porcelain.

24 Arranging a stamp collection by the size of the stamps is less common than other methods.

25 Someone who collects unusual objects may want others to think he or she is also unusual.

26 Collecting gives a feeling that other hobbies are unlikely to inspire.

READING PASSAGE 3

*You should spend about 20 minutes on **Questions 27–40**, which are based on Reading Passage 3 on pages 24 and 25.*

Questions 27–32

Reading Passage 3 has six sections, **A–F**.

Choose the correct heading for each section from the list of headings below.

*Write the correct number, **i–viii**, in boxes 27–32 on your answer sheet.*

List of Headings
i   Courses that require a high level of commitment
ii   A course title with two meanings
iii   The equal importance of two key issues
iv   Applying a theory in an unexpected context
v   The financial benefits of studying
vi   A surprising course title
vii   Different names for different outcomes
viii   The possibility of attracting the wrong kind of student

27   Section **A**

28   Section **B**

29   Section **C**

30   Section **D**

31   Section **E**

32   Section **F**

What's the purpose of gaining knowledge?

A   'I would found an institution where any person can find instruction in any subject.' That was the founder's motto for Cornell University, and it seems an apt characterization of the different university, also in the USA, where I currently teach philosophy. A student can prepare for a career in resort management, engineering, interior design, accounting, music, law enforcement, you name it. But what would the founders of these two institutions have thought of a course called 'Arson for Profit'? I kid you not: we have it on the books. Any undergraduates who have met the academic requirements can sign up for the course in our program in 'fire science'.

B   Naturally, the course is intended for prospective arson investigators, who can learn all the tricks of the trade for detecting whether a fire was deliberately set, discovering who did it, and establishing a chain of evidence for effective prosecution in a court of law. But wouldn't this also be the perfect course for prospective arsonists to sign up for? My point is not to criticize academic programs in fire science: they are highly welcome as part of the increasing professionalization of this and many other occupations. However, it's not unknown for a firefighter to torch a building. This example suggests how dishonest and illegal behavior, with the help of higher education, can creep into every aspect of public and business life.

C   I realized this anew when I was invited to speak before a class in marketing, which is another of our degree programs. The regular instructor is a colleague who appreciates the kind of ethical perspective I can bring as a philosopher. There are endless ways I could have approached this assignment, but I took my cue from the title of the course: 'Principles of Marketing'. It made me think to ask the students, 'Is marketing principled?' After all, a subject matter can have principles in the sense of being codified, having rules, as with football or chess, without being principled in the sense of being ethical. Many of the students immediately assumed that the answer to my question about marketing principles was obvious: *no.* Just look at the ways in which everything under the sun has been marketed; obviously it need not be done in a *principled* (=ethical) fashion.

D   Is that obvious? I made the suggestion, which may sound downright crazy in light of the evidence, that perhaps marketing is *by definition* principled. My inspiration for this judgement is the philosopher Immanuel Kant, who argued that any body of knowledge consists of an end (or purpose) and a means.

E   Let us apply both the terms 'means' and 'end' to marketing. The students have signed up for a course in order to learn how to market effectively. But to what *end*? There seem to be two main attitudes toward that question. One is that the answer is obvious: the purpose of marketing is to sell things and to make money. The other attitude is that the *purpose* of marketing is irrelevant: Each person comes to the program and course with his or her own plans, and these need not even concern the acquisition of marketing expertise as such. My proposal, which I believe would also be Kant's, is that *neither* of these attitudes captures the significance of the end to the means for marketing. A field of knowledge or a professional endeavor is defined by both the means *and* the end; hence *both* deserve scrutiny. Students need to study both how to achieve X, and also what X is.

F   It is at this point that 'Arson for Profit' becomes supremely relevant. That course is presumably all about *means*: how to detect and prosecute criminal activity. It is therefore assumed that the *end* is good in an ethical sense. When I ask fire science students to articulate the end, or purpose, of their field, they eventually generalize to something like, 'The safety and welfare of society,' which seems right. As we have seen, someone could use the very same knowledge of *means* to achieve a much less noble end, such as personal profit via destructive, dangerous, reckless activity. But *we would not call that firefighting*. We have a separate word for it: *arson*. Similarly, if you employed the 'principles of marketing' in an unprincipled way, *you would not be doing marketing*. We have another term for it: *fraud*. Kant gives the example of a doctor and a poisoner, who use the identical knowledge to achieve their divergent ends. We would say that one is practicing medicine, the other, murder.

Questions 33–36

Complete the summary below.

*Choose **NO MORE THAN TWO WORDS** from the passage for each answer.*

Write your answers in boxes 33–36 on your answer sheet.

The 'Arson for Profit' course

This is a university course intended for students who are undergraduates and who are studying **33** ………… . The expectation is that they will become **34** ………… specialising in arson. The course will help them to detect cases of arson and find **35** ………… of criminal intent, leading to successful **36** ………… in the courts.

Questions 37–40

Do the following statements agree with the views of the writer in Reading Passage 3?

In boxes 37–40 on your answer sheet, write

> **YES**   *if the statement agrees with the views of the writer*
> **NO**   *if the statement contradicts the views of the writer*
> **NOT GIVEN** *if it is impossible to say what the writer thinks about this*

37 It is difficult to attract students onto courses that do not focus on a career.

38 The 'Arson for Profit' course would be useful for people intending to set fire to buildings.

39 Fire science courses are too academic to help people to be good at the job of firefighting.

40 The writer's fire science students provided a detailed definition of the purpose of their studies.

WRITING

WRITING TASK 1

You should spend about 20 minutes on this task.

The bar chart below shows the percentage of Australian men and women in different age groups who did regular physical activity in 2010.

Summarise the information by selecting and reporting the main features, and make comparisons where relevant.

Write at least 150 words.

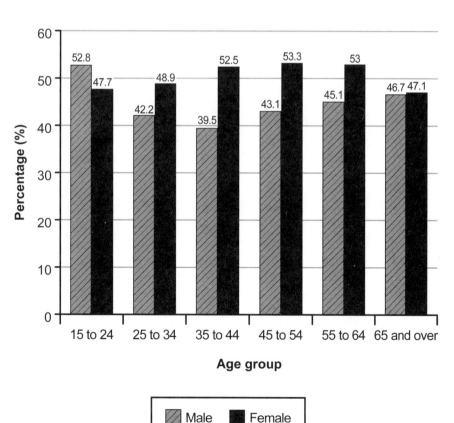

Percentage of Australian men and women doing regular physical activity: 2010

WRITING TASK 2

You should spend about 40 minutes on this task.

Write about the following topic:

Some people believe that it is good to share as much information as possible in scientific research, business and the academic world. Others believe that some information is too important or too valuable to be shared freely.

Discuss both these views and give your own opinion.

Give reasons for your answer and include any relevant examples from your own knowledge or experience.

Write at least 250 words.

SPEAKING

PART 1

The examiner asks the candidate about him/herself, his/her home, work or studies and other familiar topics.

EXAMPLE

Health

• Is it important to you to eat healthy food? [Why?/Why not?]
• If you catch a cold, what do you do to help you feel better? [Why?]
• Do you pay attention to public information about health? [Why?/Why not?]
• What could you do to have a healthier lifestyle?

PART 2

Describe an occasion when you had to wait a long time for someone or something to arrive.

You should say:
    who or what you were waiting for
    how long you had to wait
    why you had to wait a long time
and explain how you felt about waiting a long time.

You will have to talk about the topic for one to two minutes. You have one minute to think about what you are going to say. You can make some notes to help you if you wish.

PART 3

Discussion topics:

Arriving early

Example questions:
In what kinds of situations should people always arrive early?
How important it is to arrive early in your country?
How can modern technology help people to arrive early?

Being patient

Example questions:
What kinds of jobs require the most patience?
Is it always better to be patient in work (or studies)?
Do you agree or disagree that the older people are, the more patient they are?

Test 6

LISTENING

SECTION 1   *Questions 1–10*

Complete the notes below.

Write **ONE WORD AND/OR A NUMBER** for each answer.

Events during Kenton Festival

Example

Start date: ....16th.......... May

Opening ceremony (first day)

- In town centre, starting at **1** ....

  The mayor will make a speech

  A **2** .... will perform

  Performance of a **3** .... about Helen Tungate (a **4** ....)

  Evening fireworks display situated across the **5** ....

Other events

- Videos about relationships that children have with their **6** ....

  Venue: **7** .... House

- Performance of **8** .... dances

  Venue: the **9** .... market in the town centre

  Time: 2 and 5 pm every day except 1st day of festival

- Several professional concerts and one by children
  Venue: library
  Time: 6.30 pm on the 18th

  Tickets available online from festival box office and from shops which have the festival **10** .... in their windows

---

SECTION 2   *Questions 11–20*

Questions 11–15

*Choose the correct letter, **A**, **B** or **C**.*

Theatre trip to Munich

11   When the group meet at the airport they will have

    A   breakfast.
    B   coffee.
    C   lunch.

12   The group will be met at Munich Airport by

    A   an employee at the National Theatre.
    B   a theatre manager.
    C   a tour operator.

13   How much will they pay per night for a double room at the hotel?

    A   110 euros
    B   120 euros
    C   150 euros

14   What type of restaurant will they go to on Tuesday evening?

    A   an Italian restaurant
    B   a Lebanese restaurant
    C   a typical restaurant of the region

15   Who will they meet on Wednesday afternoon?

    A   an actor
    B   a playwright
    C   a theatre director

Questions 16–20

What does the man say about the play on each of the following days?

*Choose **FIVE** answers from the box and write the correct letter, **A–G**, next to Questions 16–20.*

Comments
A   The playwright will be present.
B   The play was written to celebrate an anniversary.
C   The play will be performed inside a historic building.
D   The play will be accompanied by live music.
E   The play will be performed outdoors.
F   The play will be performed for the first time.
G   The performance will be attended by officials from the town.

Days

16 Wednesday   ....

17 Thursday   ....

18 Friday   ....

19 Saturday   ....

20 Monday   ....

SECTION 3   *Questions 21–30*

Questions 21–25

*Choose the correct letter, **A**, **B** or **C**.*

Scandinavian Studies

21   James chose to take Scandinavian Studies because when he was a child

    A   he was often taken to Denmark.
    B   his mother spoke to him in Danish.
    C   a number of Danish people visited his family.

22   When he graduates, James would like to

    A   take a postgraduate course.
    B   work in the media.
    C   become a translator.

23   Which course will end this term?

    A   Swedish cinema
    B   Danish television programmes
    C   Scandinavian literature

24   They agree that James's literature paper this term will be on

    A   19th century playwrights.
    B   the Icelandic sagas.
    C   modern Scandinavian novels.

25   Beth recommends that James's paper should be

    A   a historical overview of the genre.
    B   an in-depth analysis of a single writer.
    C   a study of the social background to the literature.

Questions 26–30

Complete the flow-chart below.

*Choose **FIVE** answers from the box and write the correct letter, **A–G**, next to Questions 26–30.*

A	bullet points
B	film
C	notes
D	structure
E	student paper
F	textbook
G	documentary

How James will write his paper on the Vikings

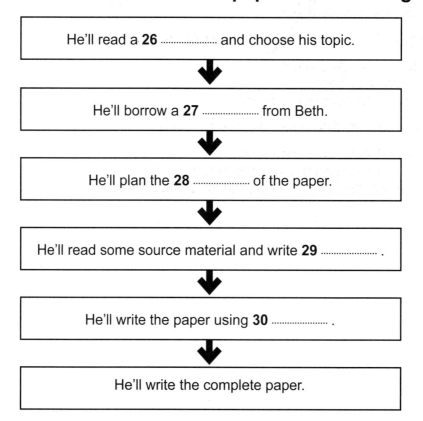

He'll read a **26** .... and choose his topic.

He'll borrow a **27** .... from Beth.

He'll plan the **28** .... of the paper.

He'll read some source material and write **29** ....

He'll write the paper using **30** ....

He'll write the complete paper.

SECTION 4   *Questions 31–40*

Complete the notes below.

Write **ONE WORD ONLY** *for each answer.*

Conflict at work

Conflict mostly consists of behaviour in the general category of **31** ....

Often a result of people wanting to prove their **32** ....

Also caused by differences in **33** .... between people

34 '..................................' conflicts: people more concerned about own team than about company

Conflict-related stress can cause **35** .... that may last for months

Chief Executives (CEOs)

Many have both **36** .... and anxiety

May not like to have their decisions questioned

There may be conflict between people who have different **37** ....

Other managers

A structure that is more **38** .... may create a feeling of uncertainty about who staff should report to.

Minimising conflict

Bosses need to try hard to gain **39** ....

Someone from outside the company may be given the role of **40** .... in order to resolve conflicts.

READING

READING PASSAGE 1

*You should spend about 20 minutes on **Questions 1–13**, which are based on Reading Passage 1 below.*

The risks agriculture faces in developing countries

*Synthesis of an online debate**

A   Two things distinguish food production from all other productive activities: first, every single person needs food each day and has a right to it; and second, it is hugely dependent on nature. These two unique aspects, one political, the other natural, make food production highly vulnerable and different from any other business. At the same time, cultural values are highly entrenched in food and agricultural systems worldwide.

B   Farmers everywhere face major risks, including extreme weather, long-term climate change, and price volatility in input and product markets. However, smallholder farmers in developing countries must in addition deal with adverse environments, both natural, in terms of soil quality, rainfall, etc., and human, in terms of infrastructure, financial systems, markets, knowledge and technology. Counter-intuitively, hunger is prevalent among many smallholder farmers in the developing world.

C   Participants in the online debate argued that our biggest challenge is to address the underlying causes of the agricultural system's inability to ensure sufficient food for all, and they identified as drivers of this problem our dependency on fossil fuels and unsupportive government policies.

D   On the question of mitigating the risks farmers face, most essayists called for greater state intervention. In his essay, Kanayo F. Nwanze, President of the International Fund for Agricultural Development, argued that governments can significantly reduce risks for farmers by providing basic services like roads to get produce more efficiently to markets, or water and food storage facilities to reduce losses. Sophia Murphy, senior advisor to the Institute for Agriculture and Trade Policy, suggested that the procurement and holding of stocks by governments can also help mitigate wild swings in food prices by alleviating uncertainties about market supply.

---

*The personal names in the text refer to the authors of written contributions to the online debate.

E   Shenggen Fan, Director General of the International Food Policy Research Institute, held up social safety nets and public welfare programmes in Ethiopia, Brazil and Mexico as valuable ways to address poverty among farming families and reduce their vulnerability to agriculture shocks. However, some commentators responded that cash transfers to poor families do not necessarily translate into increased food security, as these programmes do not always strengthen food production or raise incomes. Regarding state subsidies for agriculture, Rokeya Kabir, Executive Director of Bangladesh Nari Progati Sangha, commented in her essay that these 'have not compensated for the stranglehold exercised by private traders. In fact, studies show that sixty percent of beneficiaries of subsidies are not poor, but rich landowners and non-farmer traders.'

F   Nwanze, Murphy and Fan argued that private risk management tools, like private insurance, commodity futures markets, and rural finance can help small-scale producers mitigate risk and allow for investment in improvements. Kabir warned that financial support schemes often encourage the adoption of high-input agricultural practices, which in the medium term may raise production costs beyond the value of their harvests. Murphy noted that when futures markets become excessively financialised they can contribute to short-term price volatility, which increases farmers' food insecurity. Many participants and commentators emphasised that greater transparency in markets is needed to mitigate the impact of volatility, and make evident whether adequate stocks and supplies are available. Others contended that agribusiness companies should be held responsible for paying for negative side effects.

G   Many essayists mentioned climate change and its consequences for small-scale agriculture. Fan explained that 'in addition to reducing crop yields, climate change increases the magnitude and the frequency of extreme weather events, which increase smallholder vulnerability.' The growing unpredictability of weather patterns increases farmers' difficulty in managing weather-related risks. According to this author, one solution would be to develop crop varieties that are more resilient to new climate trends and extreme weather patterns. Accordingly, Pat Mooney, co-founder and executive director of the ETC Group, suggested that 'if we are to survive climate change, we must adopt policies that let peasants diversify the plant and animal species and varieties/breeds that make up our menus.'

H   Some participating authors and commentators argued in favour of community-based and autonomous risk management strategies through collective action groups, co-operatives or producers' groups. Such groups enhance market opportunities for small-scale producers, reduce marketing costs and synchronise buying and selling with seasonal price conditions. According to Murphy, 'collective action offers an important way for farmers to strengthen their political and economic bargaining power, and to reduce their business risks.' One commentator, Giel Ton, warned that collective action does not come as a free good. It takes time, effort and money to organise, build trust and to experiment. Others, like Marcel Vernooij and Marcel Beukeboom, suggested that in order to 'apply what we already know', all stakeholders, including business, government, scientists and civil society, must work together, starting at the beginning of the value chain.

I   Some participants explained that market price volatility is often worsened by the presence of intermediary purchasers who, taking advantage of farmers' vulnerability, dictate prices. One commentator suggested farmers can gain greater control over prices and minimise price volatility by selling directly to consumers. Similarly, Sonali Bisht, founder and advisor to the Institute of Himalayan Environmental Research and Education (INHERE), India, wrote that community-supported agriculture, where consumers invest in local farmers by subscription and guarantee producers a fair price, is a risk-sharing model worth more attention. Direct food distribution systems not only encourage small-scale agriculture but also give consumers more control over the food they consume, she wrote.

Questions 1–3

Reading Passage 1 has nine paragraphs, **A–I**.

Which paragraph contains the following information?

*Write the correct letter, **A–I**, in boxes 1–3 on your answer sheet.*

1   a reference to characteristics that only apply to food production

2   a reference to challenges faced only by farmers in certain parts of the world

3   a reference to difficulties in bringing about co-operation between farmers

Questions 4–9

Look at the following statements (Questions 4–9) and the list of people below.

*Match each statement with the correct person, **A–G**.*

*Write the correct letter, **A–G**, in boxes 4–9 on your answer sheet.*

NB *You may use any letter more than once.*

4   Financial assistance from the government does not always go to the farmers who
      most need it.

5   Farmers can benefit from collaborating as a group.

6   Financial assistance from the government can improve the standard of living of
      farmers.

7   Farmers may be helped if there is financial input by the same individuals who buy
      from them.

8   Governments can help to reduce variation in prices.

9   Improvements to infrastructure can have a major impact on risk for farmers.

	List of People
A	Kanayo F. Nwanze
B	Sophia Murphy
C	Shenggen Fan
D	Rokeya Kabir
E	Pat Mooney
F	Giel Ton
G	Sonali Bisht

Questions 10 and 11

*Choose **TWO** letters, **A–E**.*

Write the correct letters in boxes 10 and 11 on your answer sheet.

Which **TWO** problems are mentioned which affect farmers with small farms in developing countries?

    A   lack of demand for locally produced food
    B   lack of irrigation programmes
    C   being unable to get insurance
    D   the effects of changing weather patterns
    E   having to sell their goods to intermediary buyers

Questions 12 and 13

*Choose **TWO** letters, **A–E**.*

Write the correct letters in boxes 12 and 13 on your answer sheet.

Which **TWO** actions are recommended for improving conditions for farmers?

    A   reducing the size of food stocks
    B   attempting to ensure that prices rise at certain times of the year
    C   organising co-operation between a wide range of interested parties
    D   encouraging consumers to take a financial stake in farming
    E   making customers aware of the reasons for changing food prices

READING PASSAGE 2

*You should spend about 20 minutes on **Questions 14–26**, which are based on Reading Passage 2 below.*

Questions 14–20

Reading Passage 2 has seven paragraphs, **A–G**.

Choose the correct heading for each paragraph from the list of headings below.

*Write the correct number, **i–viii**, in boxes 14–20 on your answer sheet.*

List of Headings
i   Different accounts of the same journey
ii   Bingham gains support
iii   A common belief
iv   The aim of the trip
v   A dramatic description
vi   A new route
vii   Bingham publishes his theory
viii Bingham's lack of enthusiasm

14   Paragraph **A**

15   Paragraph **B**

16   Paragraph **C**

17   Paragraph **D**

18   Paragraph **E**

19   Paragraph **F**

20   Paragraph **G**

The Lost City

An explorer's encounter with the ruined city of Machu Picchu, the most famous icon of the Inca civilisation

A　When the US explorer and academic Hiram Bingham arrived in South America in 1911, he was ready for what was to be the greatest achievement of his life: the exploration of the remote hinterland to the west of Cusco, the old capital of the Inca empire in the Andes mountains of Peru. His goal was to locate the remains of a city called Vitcos, the last capital of the Inca civilisation. Cusco lies on a high plateau at an elevation of more than 3,000 metres, and Bingham's plan was to descend from this plateau along the valley of the Urubamba river, which takes a circuitous route down to the Amazon and passes through an area of dramatic canyons and mountain ranges.

B　When Bingham and his team set off down the Urubamba in late July, they had an advantage over travellers who had preceded them: a track had recently been blasted down the valley canyon to enable rubber to be brought up by mules from the jungle. Almost all previous travellers had left the river at Ollantaytambo and taken a high pass across the mountains to rejoin the river lower down, thereby cutting a substantial corner, but also therefore never passing through the area around Machu Picchu.

C　On 24 July they were a few days into their descent of the valley. The day began slowly, with Bingham trying to arrange sufficient mules for the next stage of the trek. His companions showed no interest in accompanying him up the nearby hill to see some ruins that a local farmer, Melchor Arteaga, had told them about the night before. The morning was dull and damp, and Bingham also seems to have been less than keen on the prospect of climbing the hill. In his book *Lost City of the Incas*, he relates that he made the ascent without having the least expectation that he would find anything at the top.

D　Bingham writes about the approach in vivid style in his book. First, as he climbs up the hill, he describes the ever-present possibility of deadly snakes, 'capable of making considerable springs when in pursuit of their prey'; not that he sees any. Then there's a sense of mounting discovery as he comes across great sweeps of terraces, then a mausoleum, followed by monumental staircases and, finally, the grand ceremonial buildings of Machu Picchu. 'It seemed like an unbelievable dream … the sight held me spellbound …' he wrote.

E   We should remember, however, that *Lost City of the Incas* is a work of hindsight, not written until 1948, many years after his journey. His journal entries of the time reveal a much more gradual appreciation of his achievement. He spent the afternoon at the ruins noting down the dimensions of some of the buildings, then descended and rejoined his companions, to whom he seems to have said little about his discovery. At this stage, Bingham didn't realise the extent or the importance of the site, nor did he realise what use he could make of the discovery.

F   However, soon after returning it occurred to him that he could make a name for himself from this discovery. When he came to write the National Geographic magazine article that broke the story to the world in April 1913, he knew he had to produce a big idea. He wondered whether it could have been the birthplace of the very first Inca, Manco the Great, and whether it could also have been what chroniclers described as 'the last city of the Incas'. This term refers to Vilcabamba, the settlement where the Incas had fled from Spanish invaders in the 1530s. Bingham made desperate attempts to prove this belief for nearly 40 years. Sadly, his vision of the site as both the beginning and end of the Inca civilisation, while a magnificent one, is inaccurate. We now know that Vilcabamba actually lies 65 kilometres away in the depths of the jungle.

G   One question that has perplexed visitors, historians and archaeologists alike ever since Bingham, is why the site seems to have been abandoned before the Spanish Conquest. There are no references to it by any of the Spanish chroniclers – and if they had known of its existence so close to Cusco they would certainly have come in search of gold. An idea which has gained wide acceptance over the past few years is that Machu Picchu was a *moya*, a country estate built by an Inca emperor to escape the cold winters of Cusco, where the elite could enjoy monumental architecture and spectacular views. Furthermore, the particular architecture of Machu Picchu suggests that it was constructed at the time of the greatest of all the Incas, the emperor Pachacuti (c. 1438–71). By custom, Pachacuti's descendants built other similar estates for their own use, and so Machu Picchu would have been abandoned after his death, some 50 years before the Spanish Conquest.

Questions 21–24

Do the following statements agree with the information given in Reading Passage 2?

In boxes 21–24 on your answer sheet, write

> **TRUE**   *if the statement agrees with the information*
> **FALSE**   *if the statement contradicts the information*
> **NOT GIVEN**   *if there is no information on this*

21   Bingham went to South America in search of an Inca city.

22   Bingham chose a particular route down the Urubamba valley because it was the most common route used by travellers.

23   Bingham understood the significance of Machu Picchu as soon as he saw it.

24   Bingham returned to Machu Picchu in order to find evidence to support his theory.

Questions 25–26

Complete the sentences below.

*Choose **ONE WORD ONLY** from the passage for each answer.*

Write your answers in boxes 25–26 on your answer sheet.

25   The track that took Bingham down the Urubamba valley had been created for the transportation of ....

26   Bingham found out about the ruins of Machu Picchu from a .... in the Urubamba valley.

READING PASSAGE 3

*You should spend about 20 minutes on **Questions 27–40**, which are based on Reading Passage 3 below.*

The Benefits of Being Bilingual

A   According to the latest figures, the majority of the world's population is now bilingual or multilingual, having grown up speaking two or more languages. In the past, such children were considered to be at a disadvantage compared with their monolingual peers. Over the past few decades, however, technological advances have allowed researchers to look more deeply at how bilingualism interacts with and changes the cognitive and neurological systems, thereby identifying several clear benefits of being bilingual.

B   Research shows that when a bilingual person uses one language, the other is active at the same time. When we hear a word, we don't hear the entire word all at once: the sounds arrive in sequential order. Long before the word is finished, the brain's language system begins to guess what that word might be. If you hear 'can', you will likely activate words like 'candy' and 'candle' as well, at least during the earlier stages of word recognition. For bilingual people, this activation is not limited to a single language; auditory input activates corresponding words regardless of the language to which they belong. Some of the most compelling evidence for this phenomenon, called 'language co-activation', comes from studying eye movements. A Russian-English bilingual asked to 'pick up a marker' from a set of objects would look more at a stamp than someone who doesn't know Russian, because the Russian word for 'stamp', *marka*, sounds like the English word he or she heard, 'marker'. In cases like this, language co-activation occurs because what the listener hears could map onto words in either language.

C   Having to deal with this persistent linguistic competition can result in difficulties, however. For instance, knowing more than one language can cause speakers to name pictures more slowly, and can increase 'tip-of-the-tongue states', when you can almost, but not quite, bring a word to mind. As a result, the constant juggling of two languages creates a need to control how much a person accesses a language at any given time. For this reason, bilingual people often perform better on tasks that require conflict management. In the classic Stroop Task, people see a word and are asked to name the colour of the word's font. When the colour and the word match (i.e., the word 'red' printed in red), people correctly name the colour more quickly than when the colour and the word don't match (i.e., the word 'red' printed in blue). This occurs because the word itself ('red') and its font colour (blue) conflict. Bilingual people often excel at tasks such as this, which tap into the ability to ignore competing perceptual information and focus on the relevant aspects of the input. Bilinguals are also better at switching between two tasks; for example, when bilinguals have to switch from categorizing objects by colour (red or green) to categorizing them by shape (circle or triangle), they do so more quickly than monolingual people, reflecting better cognitive control when having to make rapid changes of strategy.

D It also seems that the neurological roots of the bilingual advantage extend to brain areas more traditionally associated with sensory processing. When monolingual and bilingual adolescents listen to simple speech sounds without any intervening background noise, they show highly similar brain stem responses. When researchers play the same sound to both groups in the presence of background noise, however, the bilingual listeners' neural response is considerably larger, reflecting better encoding of the sound's fundamental frequency, a feature of sound closely related to pitch perception.

E Such improvements in cognitive and sensory processing may help a bilingual person to process information in the environment, and help explain why bilingual adults acquire a third language better than monolingual adults master a second language. This advantage may be rooted in the skill of focussing on information about the new language while reducing interference from the languages they already know.

F Research also indicates that bilingual experience may help to keep the cognitive mechanisms sharp by recruiting alternate brain networks to compensate for those that become damaged during aging. Older bilinguals enjoy improved memory relative to monolingual people, which can lead to real-world health benefits. In a study of over 200 patients with Alzheimer's disease, a degenerative brain disease, bilingual patients reported showing initial symptoms of the disease an average of five years later than monolingual patients. In a follow-up study, researchers compared the brains of bilingual and monolingual patients matched on the severity of Alzheimer's symptoms. Surprisingly, the bilinguals' brains had more physical signs of disease than their monolingual counterparts, even though their outward behaviour and abilities were the same. If the brain is an engine, bilingualism may help it to go farther on the same amount of fuel.

G Furthermore, the benefits associated with bilingual experience seem to start very early. In one study, researchers taught seven-month-old babies growing up in monolingual or bilingual homes that when they heard a tinkling sound, a puppet appeared on one side of a screen. Halfway through the study, the puppet began appearing on the opposite side of the screen. In order to get a reward, the infants had to adjust the rule they'd learned; only the bilingual babies were able to successfully learn the new rule. This suggests that for very young children, as well as for older people, navigating a multilingual environment imparts advantages that transfer far beyond language.

Questions 27–31

Complete the table below.

Choose **NO MORE THAN TWO WORDS** from the passage for each answer.

Write your answers in boxes 27–31 on your answer sheet.

Test	Findings
Observing the 27 .... of Russian-English bilingual people when asked to select certain objects	Bilingual people engage both languages simultaneously: a mechanism known as 28 ....
A test called the 29 .... , focusing on naming colours	Bilingual people are more able to handle tasks involving a skill called 30 ....
A test involving switching between tasks	When changing strategies, bilingual people have superior 31 ....

Questions 32–36

Do the following statements agree with the claims of the writer in Reading Passage 3?

In boxes 32–36 on your answer sheet, write

> **YES** if the statement agrees with the claims of the writer
> **NO** if the statement contradicts the claims of the writer
> **NOT GIVEN** if it is impossible to say what the writer thinks about this

32 Attitudes towards bilingualism have changed in recent years.

33 Bilingual people are better than monolingual people at guessing correctly what words are before they are finished.

34 Bilingual people consistently name images faster than monolingual people.

35 Bilingual people's brains process single sounds more efficiently than monolingual people in all situations.

36 Fewer bilingual people than monolingual people suffer from brain disease in old age.

Questions 37–40

Reading Passage 3 has seven paragraphs, **A–G**.

Which paragraph contains the following information?

*Write the correct letter, **A–G**, in boxes 37–40 on your answer sheet.*

37 an example of how bilingual and monolingual people's brains respond differently to a certain type of non-verbal auditory input

38 a demonstration of how a bilingual upbringing has benefits even before we learn to speak

39 a description of the process by which people identify words that they hear

40 reference to some negative consequences of being bilingual

WRITING

WRITING TASK 1

You should spend about 20 minutes on this task.

> **The maps below show the centre of a small town called Islip as it is now, and plans for its development.**
>
> **Summarise the information by selecting and reporting the main features, and make comparisons where relevant.**

Write at least 150 words.

Islip town centre now

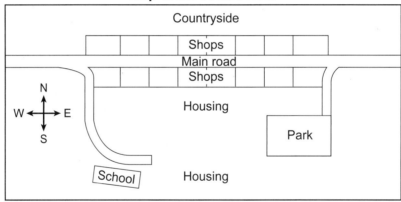

Islip town centre: planned development

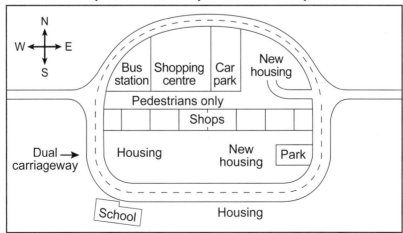

WRITING TASK 2

You should spend about 40 minutes on this task.

Write about the following topic:

> **At the present time, the population of some countries includes a relatively large number of young adults, compared with the number of older people.**
>
> **Do the advantages of this situation outweigh the disadvantages?**

Give reasons for your answer and include any relevant examples from your own knowledge or experience.

Write at least 250 words.

SPEAKING

PART 1

The examiner asks the candidate about him/herself, his/her home, work or studies and other familiar topics.

EXAMPLE

Songs and singing

- Did you enjoy singing when you were younger? [Why?/Why not?]
- How often do you sing now? [Why?]
- Do you have a favourite song you like listening to? [Why?/Why not?]
- How important is singing in your culture? [Why?]

PART 2

Describe a film/movie actor from your country who is very popular.
 	
You should say:
      who this actor is
      what kinds of films/movies he/she acts in
      what you know about this actor's life
and explain why this actor is so popular.

You will have to talk about the topic for one to two minutes. You have one minute to think about what you are going to say. You can make some notes to help you if you wish.

PART 3

Discussion topics:

Watching films/movies

Example questions:
What are the most popular types of films in your country?
What is the difference between watching a film in the cinema and watching a film at home?
Do you think cinemas will close in the future?

Theatre

Example questions:
How important is the theatre in your country's history?
How strong a tradition is it today in your country to go to the theatre?
Do you think the theatre should be run as a business or as a public service?

Test 7

SECTION 1   *Questions 1–10*

Complete the notes below.

Write **ONE WORD ONLY** for each answer.

PUBLIC LIBRARY

Example

The library re-opened last ....month............

The library now has

- a seating area with magazines
- an expanded section for books on **1** ....
- a new section on local **2** ....
- a community room for meetings (also possible to **3** .... there)
- a new section of books for **4** ....

For younger children

- the next Science Club meeting: experiments using things from your
  5 ....
- Reading Challenge: read six books during the holidays

For adults

- this Friday: a local author talks about a novel based on a real **6** ....
- IT support is available on Tuesdays – no **7** .... is necessary
- free check of blood **8** .... and cholesterol levels (over 60s only)

Other information

- the library shop sells wall-charts, cards and **9** ....
- evenings and weekends: free **10** .... is available

---

SECTION 2   *Questions 11–20*

Questions 11 and 12

*Choose **TWO** letters, **A–E**.*

Which **TWO** age groups are taking increasing numbers of holidays with BC Travel?

    A   16–30 years
    B   31–42 years
    C   43–54 years
    D   55–64 years
    E   over 65 years

Questions 13 and 14

*Choose **TWO** letters, **A–E**.*

Which **TWO** are the main reasons given for the popularity of activity holidays?

    A   Clients make new friends.
    B   Clients learn a useful skill.
    C   Clients learn about a different culture.
    D   Clients are excited by the risk involved.
    E   Clients find them good value for money.

Questions 15–17

*Choose the correct letter, **A**, **B** or **C**.*

15   How does BC Travel plan to expand the painting holidays?

    A   by adding to the number of locations
    B   by increasing the range of levels
    C   by employing more teachers

16   Why are BC Travel's cooking holidays unusual?

    A   They only use organic foods.
    B   They have an international focus.
    C   They mainly involve vegetarian dishes.

17   What does the speaker say about the photography holidays?

    A   Clients receive individual tuition.
    B   The tutors are also trained guides.
    C   Advice is given on selling photographs.

Listening

Questions 18–20

Complete the table below.

*Write **ONE WORD ONLY** for each answer.*

Fitness Holidays

Location	Main focus	Other comments
Ireland and Italy	general fitness	• personally designed programme • also reduces **18** ....
Greece	**19** .... control	• includes exercise on the beach
Morocco	mountain biking	• wide variety of levels • one holiday that is specially designed for **20** ....

SECTION 3 *Questions 21–30*

Questions 21–26

Complete the flow-chart below.

*Choose **SIX** answers from the box and write the correct letter, **A–H**, next to Questions 21–26.*

A patterns	**B** names	**C** sources	**D** questions
E employees	**F** solutions	**G** headings	**H** officials

STAGES IN DOING A TOURISM CASE STUDY

RESEARCH

Locate and read relevant articles, noting key information and also **21** ....
Identify a problem or need

Select interviewees – these may be site **22** .... , visitors or
city **23** ....

Prepare and carry out interviews. If possible, collect statistics.

Check whether **24** .... of interviewees can be used

ANALYSIS

Select relevant information and try to identify **25** ....

Decide on the best form of visuals

WRITING THE CASE STUDY

Give some background before writing the main sections

Do NOT end with **26** ....

Questions 27–30

*Choose the correct letter, **A**, **B** or **C**.*

The Horton Castle site

27   Natalie and Dave agree one reason why so few people visit Horton Castle is that

    A   the publicity is poor.
    B   it is difficult to get to.
    C   there is little there of interest.

28   Natalie and Dave agree that the greatest problem with a visitor centre could be

    A   covering the investment costs.
    B   finding a big enough space for it.
    C   dealing with planning restrictions.

29   What does Dave say about conditions in the town of Horton?

    A   There is a lot of unemployment.
    B   There are few people of working age.
    C   There are opportunities for skilled workers.

30   According to Natalie, one way to prevent damage to the castle site would be to

    A   insist visitors have a guide.
    B   make visitors keep to the paths.
    C   limit visitor numbers.

SECTION 4   *Questions 31–40*

Complete the notes below.

*Write **ONE WORD ONLY** for each answer.*

The effects of environmental change on birds

Mercury (Hg)

- Highly toxic

- Released into the atmosphere from coal

- In water it may be consumed by fish

- It has also recently been found to affect birds which feed on **31** ....

Research on effects of mercury on birds

- Claire Varian-Ramos is investigating:

  – the effects on birds' **32** .... or mental processes, e.g. memory

  – the effects on bird song (usually learned from a bird's **33** ....)

- Findings:

  – songs learned by birds exposed to mercury are less **34** ....

  – this may have a negative effect on birds' **35** ....

- Lab-based studies:

  – allow more **36** .... for the experimenter

Implications for humans

- Migrating birds such as **37** .... containing mercury may be eaten by humans

- Mercury also causes problems in learning **38** ....

- Mercury in a mother's body from **39** .... may affect the unborn child

- New regulations for mercury emissions will affect everyone's energy **40** ....

READING

READING PASSAGE 1

*You should spend about 20 minutes on **Questions 1–13**, which are based on Reading Passage 1.*

Questions 1–7

Reading Passage 1 has seven paragraphs, **A–G**.

Choose the correct heading for each paragraph from the list of headings below.

*Write the correct number, **i–viii**, in boxes 1–7 on your answer sheet.*

List of Headings

i	The importance of getting the timing right
ii	Young meets old
iii	Developments to the disadvantage of tortoise populations
iv	Planning a bigger idea
v	Tortoises populate the islands
vi	Carrying out a carefully prepared operation
vii	Looking for a home for the islands' tortoises
viii	The start of the conservation project

---

1   Paragraph **A**

2   Paragraph **B**

3   Paragraph **C**

4   Paragraph **D**

5   Paragraph **E**

6   Paragraph **F**

7   Paragraph **G**

Flying tortoises

An airborne reintroduction programme has helped conservationists take significant steps to protect the endangered Galápagos tortoise.

A   Forests of spiny cacti cover much of the uneven lava plains that separate the interior of the Galápagos island of Isabela from the Pacific Ocean. With its five distinct volcanoes, the island resembles a lunar landscape. Only the thick vegetation at the skirt of the often cloud-covered peak of Sierra Negra offers respite from the barren terrain below. This inhospitable environment is home to the giant Galápagos tortoise. Some time after the Galápagos's birth, around five million years ago, the islands were colonised by one or more tortoises from mainland South America. As these ancestral tortoises settled on the individual islands, the different populations adapted to their unique environments, giving rise to at least 14 different subspecies. Island life agreed with them. In the absence of significant predators, they grew to become the largest and longest-living tortoises on the planet, weighing more than 400 kilograms, occasionally exceeding 1.8 metres in length and living for more than a century.

B   Before human arrival, the archipelago's tortoises numbered in the hundreds of thousands. From the 17th century onwards, pirates took a few on board for food, but the arrival of whaling ships in the 1790s saw this exploitation grow exponentially. Relatively immobile and capable of surviving for months without food or water, the tortoises were taken on board these ships to act as food supplies during long ocean passages. Sometimes, their bodies were processed into high-grade oil. In total, an estimated 200,000 animals were taken from the archipelago before the 20th century. This historical exploitation was then exacerbated when settlers came to the islands. They hunted the tortoises and destroyed their habitat to clear land for agriculture. They also introduced alien species – ranging from cattle, pigs, goats, rats and dogs to plants and ants – that either prey on the eggs and young tortoises or damage or destroy their habitat.

C   Today, only 11 of the original subspecies survive and of these, several are highly endangered. In 1989, work began on a tortoise-breeding centre just outside the town of Puerto Villamil on Isabela, dedicated to protecting the island's tortoise populations. The centre's captive-breeding programme proved to be extremely successful, and it eventually had to deal with an overpopulation problem.

D   The problem was also a pressing one. Captive-bred tortoises can't be reintroduced into the wild until they're at least five years old and weigh at least 4.5 kilograms, at which point their size and weight – and their hardened shells – are sufficient to protect them from predators. But if people wait too long after that point, the tortoises eventually become too large to transport.

E   For years, repatriation efforts were carried out in small numbers, with the tortoises carried on the backs of men over weeks of long, treacherous hikes along narrow trails. But in November 2010, the environmentalist and Galápagos National Park liaison officer Godfrey Merlin, a visiting private motor yacht captain and a helicopter pilot gathered around a table in a small café in Puerto Ayora on the island of Santa Cruz to work out more ambitious reintroduction. The aim was to use a helicopter to move 300 of the breeding centre's tortoises to various locations close to Sierra Negra.

F   This unprecedented effort was made possible by the owners of the 67-metre yacht White Cloud, who provided the Galápagos National Park with free use of their helicopter and its experienced pilot, as well as the logistical support of the yacht, its captain and crew. Originally an air ambulance, the yacht's helicopter has a rear double door and a large internal space that's well suited for cargo, so a custom crate was designed to hold up to 33 tortoises with a total weight of about 150 kilograms. This weight, together with that of the fuel, pilot and four crew, approached the helicopter's maximum payload, and there were times when it was clearly right on the edge of the helicopter's capabilities. During a period of three days, a group of volunteers from the breeding centre worked around the clock to prepare the young tortoises for transport. Meanwhile, park wardens, dropped off ahead of time in remote locations, cleared landing sites within the thick brush, cacti and lava rocks.

G   Upon their release, the juvenile tortoises quickly spread out over their ancestral territory, investigating their new surroundings and feeding on the vegetation. Eventually, one tiny tortoise came across a fully grown giant who had been lumbering around the island for around a hundred years. The two stood side by side, a powerful symbol of the regeneration of an ancient species.

Questions 8–13

Complete the notes below.

*Choose **ONE WORD ONLY** from the passage for each answer.*

Write your answers in boxes 8–13 on your answer sheet.

The decline of the Galápagos tortoise

- Originally from mainland South America

- Numbers on Galápagos islands increased, due to lack of predators

- 17th century: small numbers taken onto ships used by **8** ....

- 1790s: very large numbers taken onto whaling ships, kept for **9** .... , and also used to produce **10** ....

- Hunted by **11** .... on the islands

- Habitat destruction: for the establishment of agriculture and by various **12** .... not native to the islands, which also fed on baby tortoises and tortoises' **13** ....

READING PASSAGE 2

*You should spend about 20 minutes on **Questions 14–26**, which are based on Reading Passage 2.*

The Intersection of Health Sciences and Geography

A   While many diseases that affect humans have been eradicated due to improvements in vaccinations and the availability of healthcare, there are still areas around the world where certain health issues are more prevalent. In a world that is far more globalised than ever before, people come into contact with one another through travel and living closer and closer to each other. As a result, super-viruses and other infections resistant to antibiotics are becoming more and more common.

B   Geography can often play a very large role in the health concerns of certain populations. For instance, depending on where you live, you will not have the same health concerns as someone who lives in a different geographical region. Perhaps one of the most obvious examples of this idea is malaria-prone areas, which are usually tropical regions that foster a warm and damp environment in which the mosquitos that can give people this disease can grow. Malaria is much less of a problem in high-altitude deserts, for instance.

C   In some countries, geographical factors influence the health and well-being of the population in very obvious ways. In many large cities, the wind is not strong enough to clear the air of the massive amounts of smog and pollution that cause asthma, lung problems, eyesight issues and more in the people who live there. Part of the problem is, of course, the massive number of cars being driven, in addition to factories that run on coal power. The rapid industrialisation of some countries in recent years has also led to the cutting down of forests to allow for the expansion of big cities, which makes it even harder to fight the pollution with the fresh air that is produced by plants.

D   It is in situations like these that the field of health geography comes into its own. It is an increasingly important area of study in a world where diseases like polio are re-emerging, respiratory diseases continue to spread, and malaria-prone areas are still fighting to find a better cure. Health geography is the combination of, on the one hand, knowledge regarding geography and methods used to analyse and interpret geographical information, and on the other, the study of health, diseases and healthcare practices around the world. The aim of this hybrid science is to create solutions for common geography-based health problems. While people will always be prone to illness, the study of how geography affects our health could lead to the eradication of certain illnesses, and the prevention of others in the future. By understanding why and how we get sick, we can change the way we treat illness and disease specific to certain geographical locations.

E   The geography of disease and ill health analyses the frequency with which certain diseases appear in different parts of the world, and overlays the data with the geography of the region, to see if there could be a correlation between the two. Health geographers also study factors that could make certain individuals or a population more likely to be taken ill with a specific health concern or disease, as compared with the population of another area. Health geographers in this field are usually trained as healthcare workers, and have an understanding of basic epidemiology as it relates to the spread of diseases among the population.

F   Researchers study the interactions between humans and their environment that could lead to illness (such as asthma in places with high levels of pollution) and work to create a clear way of categorising illnesses, diseases and epidemics into local and global scales. Health geographers can map the spread of illnesses and attempt to identify the reasons behind an increase or decrease in illnesses, as they work to find a way to halt the further spread or re-emergence of diseases in vulnerable populations.

G   The second subcategory of health geography is the geography of healthcare provision. This group studies the availability (or lack thereof) of healthcare resources to individuals and populations around the world. In both developed and developing nations there is often a very large discrepancy between the options available to people in different social classes, income brackets, and levels of education. Individuals working in the area of the geography of healthcare provision attempt to assess the levels of healthcare in the area (for instance, it may be very difficult for people to get medical attention because there is a mountain between their village and the nearest hospital). These researchers are on the frontline of making recommendations regarding policy to international organisations, local government bodies and others.

H   The field of health geography is often overlooked, but it constitutes a huge area of need in the fields of geography and healthcare. If we can understand how geography affects our health no matter where in the world we are located, we can better treat disease, prevent illness, and keep people safe and well.

Questions 14–19

Reading Passage 2 has eight sections, **A–H**.

Which paragraph contains the following information?

*Write the correct letter, **A–H**, in boxes 14–19 on your answer sheet.*

NB *You may use any letter more than once.*

14 an acceptance that not all diseases can be totally eliminated

15 examples of physical conditions caused by human behaviour

16 a reference to classifying diseases on the basis of how far they extend geographically

17 reasons why the level of access to healthcare can vary within a country

18 a description of health geography as a mixture of different academic fields

19 a description of the type of area where a particular illness is rare

Questions 20–26

Complete the sentences below.

*Choose **ONE WORD ONLY** from the passage for each answer.*

20 Certain diseases have disappeared, thanks to better .... and healthcare.

21 Because there is more contact between people, ... are losing their usefulness.

22 Disease-causing .... are most likely to be found in hot, damp regions.

23 One cause of pollution is .... that burn a particular fuel.

24 The growth of cities often has an impact on nearby ....

25 .... is one disease that is growing after having been eradicated.

26 A physical barrier such as a .... can prevent people from reaching a hospital.

READING PASSAGE 3

*You should spend about 20 minutes on **Questions 27–40**, which are based on Reading Passage 3.*

Music and the emotions

Neuroscientist Jonah Lehrer considers the emotional power of music

Why does music make us feel? On the one hand, music is a purely abstract art form, devoid of language or explicit ideas. And yet, even though music says little, it still manages to touch us deeply. When listening to our favourite songs, our body betrays all the symptoms of emotional arousal. The pupils in our eyes dilate, our pulse and blood pressure rise, the electrical conductance of our skin is lowered, and the cerebellum, a brain region associated with bodily movement, becomes strangely active. Blood is even re-directed to the muscles in our legs. In other words, sound stirs us at our biological roots.

A recent paper in *Nature Neuroscience* by a research team in Montreal, Canada, marks an important step in revealing the precise underpinnings of 'the potent pleasurable stimulus' that is music. Although the study involves plenty of fancy technology, including functional magnetic resonance imaging (fMRI) and ligand-based positron emission tomography (PET) scanning, the experiment itself was rather straightforward. After screening 217 individuals who responded to advertisements requesting people who experience 'chills' to instrumental music, the scientists narrowed down the subject pool to ten. They then asked the subjects to bring in their playlist of favourite songs – virtually every genre was represented, from techno to tango – and played them the music while their brain activity was monitored. Because the scientists were combining methodologies (PET and fMRI), they were able to obtain an impressively exact and detailed portrait of music in the brain. The first thing they discovered is that music triggers the production of dopamine – a chemical with a key role in setting people's moods – by the neurons (nerve cells) in both the dorsal and ventral regions of the brain. As these two regions have long been linked with the experience of pleasure, this finding isn't particularly surprising.

What is rather more significant is the finding that the dopamine neurons in the caudate – a region of the brain involved in learning stimulus-response associations, and in anticipating food and other 'reward' stimuli – were at their most active around 15 seconds before the participants' favourite moments in the music. The researchers call this the 'anticipatory phase' and argue that the purpose of this activity is to help us predict the arrival of our favourite part. The question, of course, is what all these dopamine neurons are up to. Why are they so active in the period *preceding* the acoustic climax? After all, we typically associate surges of dopamine with pleasure, with the processing of *actual* rewards. And yet, this cluster of cells is most active when the 'chills' have yet to arrive, when the melodic pattern is still unresolved.

One way to answer the question is to look at the music and not the neurons. While music can often seem (at least to the outsider) like a labyrinth of intricate patterns, it turns out that the most important part of every song or symphony is when the patterns break down, when the sound becomes unpredictable. If the music is too obvious, it is annoyingly boring, like an alarm clock. Numerous studies, after all, have demonstrated that dopamine neurons quickly adapt to predictable rewards. If we know what's going to happen next, then we don't get excited. This is why composers often introduce a key note in the beginning of a song, spend most of the rest of the piece in the studious avoidance of the pattern, and then finally repeat it only at the end. The longer we are denied the pattern we expect, the greater the emotional release when the pattern returns, safe and sound.

To demonstrate this psychological principle, the musicologist Leonard Meyer, in his classic book *Emotion and Meaning in Music* (1956), analysed the 5th movement of Beethoven's String Quartet in C-sharp minor, Op. 131. Meyer wanted to show how music is defined by its flirtation with – but not submission to – our expectations of order. Meyer dissected 50 measures (bars) of the masterpiece, showing how Beethoven begins with the clear statement of a rhythmic and harmonic pattern and then, in an ingenious tonal dance, carefully holds off repeating it. What Beethoven does instead is suggest variations of the pattern. He wants to preserve an element of uncertainty in his music, making our brains beg for the one chord he refuses to give us. Beethoven saves that chord for the end.

According to Meyer, it is the suspenseful tension of music, arising out of our unfulfilled expectations, that is the source of the music's feeling. While earlier theories of music focused on the way a sound can refer to the real world of images and experiences – its 'connotative' meaning – Meyer argued that the emotions we find in music come from the unfolding events of the music itself. This 'embodied meaning' arises from the patterns the symphony invokes and then ignores. It is this uncertainty that triggers the surge of dopamine in the caudate, as we struggle to figure out what will happen next. We can predict some of the notes, but we can't predict them all, and that is what keeps us listening, waiting expectantly for our reward, for the pattern to be completed.

Questions 27–31

Complete the summary below.

*Choose **NO MORE THAN TWO WORDS** from the passage for each answer.*

Write your answers in boxes 27–31 on your answer sheet.

The Montreal Study

Participants, who were recruited for the study through advertisements, had their brain activity monitored while listening to their favourite music. It was noted that the music stimulated the brain's neurons to release a substance called **27** .... in two of the parts of the brain which are associated with feeling **28** ....

Researchers also observed that the neurons in the area of the brain called the **29** .... were particularly active just before the participants' favourite moments in the music – the period known as the **30** .... Activity in this part of the brain is associated with the expectation of 'reward' stimuli such as **31** ....

Questions 32–36

*Choose the correct letter, **A**, **B**, **C** or **D**.*

Write the correct letter in boxes 32–36 on your answer sheet.

32 What point does the writer emphasise in the first paragraph?

   A   how dramatically our reactions to music can vary
   B   how intense our physical responses to music can be
   C   how little we know about the way that music affects us
   D   how much music can tell us about how our brains operate

33 What view of the Montreal study does the writer express in the second paragraph?

   A   Its aims were innovative.
   B   The approach was too simplistic.
   C   It produced some remarkably precise data.
   D   The technology used was unnecessarily complex.

34 What does the writer find interesting about the results of the Montreal study?

   A   the timing of participants' neural responses to the music
   B   the impact of the music on participants' emotional state
   C   the section of participants' brains which was activated by the music
   D   the type of music which had the strongest effect on participants' brains

35 Why does the writer refer to Meyer's work on music and emotion?

   A   to propose an original theory about the subject
   B   to offer support for the findings of the Montreal study
   C   to recommend the need for further research into the subject
   D   to present a view which opposes that of the Montreal researchers

36 According to Leonard Meyer, what causes the listener's emotional response to music?

   A   the way that the music evokes poignant memories in the listener
   B   the association of certain musical chords with certain feelings
   C   the listener's sympathy with the composer's intentions
   D   the internal structure of the musical composition

Test 7

Questions 37–40

*Complete each sentence with the correct ending, **A–F**, below.*

*Write the correct letter, **A–F**, in boxes 37–40 on your answer sheet.*

37 The Montreal researchers discovered that

38 Many studies have demonstrated that

39 Meyer's analysis of Beethoven's music shows that

40 Earlier theories of music suggested that

A	our response to music depends on our initial emotional state.
B	neuron activity decreases if outcomes become predictable.
C	emotive music can bring to mind actual pictures and events.
D	experiences in our past can influence our emotional reaction to music.
E	emotive music delays giving listeners what they expect to hear.
F	neuron activity increases prior to key points in a musical piece.

WRITING

WRITING TASK 1

You should spend about 20 minutes on this task.

> **The chart below shows how frequently people in the USA ate in fast food restaurants between 2003 and 2013.**
>
> **Summarise the information by selecting and reporting the main features, and make comparisons where relevant.**

Write at least 150 words.

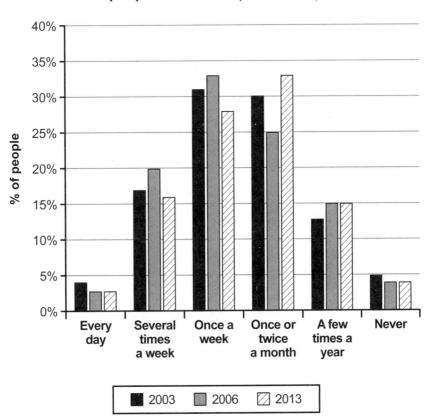

Frequency of eating at fast food restaurants among people in the USA (2003–2013)

WRITING TASK 2

You should spend about 40 minutes on this task.

Write about the following topic:

> *In a number of countries, some people think it is necessary to spend large sums of money on constructing new railway lines for very fast trains between cities. Others believe the money should be spent on improving existing public transport.*
>
> *Discuss both these views and give your own opinion.*

Give reasons for your answer and include any relevant examples from your own knowledge or experience.

Write at least 250 words.

SPEAKING

PART 1

The examiner asks the candidate about him/herself, his/her home, work or studies and other familiar topics.

EXAMPLE

Clothes

- Where do you buy most of your clothes? [Why?]
- How often do you buy new clothes for yourself? [Why?]
- How do you decide which clothes to buy? [Why?]
- Have the kinds of clothes you like changed in recent years? [Why?/Why not?]

PART 2

Describe an interesting discussion you had about how you spend your money.

You should say:
   who you had the discussion with
   why you discussed this topic
   what the result of the discussion was
and explain why this discussion was interesting for you.

You will have to talk about the topic for one to two minutes. You have one minute to think about what you are going to say. You can make some notes to help you if you wish.

PART 3

Discussion topics:

Money and young people

Example questions:
Why do some parents give their children money to spend each week?
Do you agree that schools should teach children how to manage money?
Do you think it is a good idea for students to earn money while studying?

Money and society

Example questions:
Do you think it is true that in today's society money cannot buy happiness?
What disadvantages are there in a society where the gap between rich and poor is very large?
Do you think richer countries have a responsibility to help poorer countries?

Test 8

SECTION 1   Questions 1–10

Complete the notes below.

*Write **ONE WORD AND/OR A NUMBER** for each answer.*

Cycle tour leader: Applicant enquiry

Example

Name: Margaret ....*Smith*.........

About the applicant:

• wants a **1** .... job

• will soon start work as a **2** ....

• has led cycle trips in **3** ....

• interested in being a leader of a cycling trip for families

• is currently doing voluntary work with members of a **4** .... club

• available for five months from the 1st of **5** ....

• can't eat **6** ....

Contact details:

• address: 27 **7** .... Place, Dumfries

• postcode: **8** ....

Interview:

• interview at 2.30 pm on **9** ....

• will plan a short **10** .... about being a tour guide

---

SECTION 2 *Questions 11–20*

Questions 11–14

*Choose the correct letter, **A**, **B** or **C**.*

Visiting the Sheepmarket area

11 Which is the most rapidly-growing group of residents in the Sheepmarket area?

A   young professional people
B   students from the university
C   employees in the local market

12 The speaker recommends the side streets in the Sheepmarket for their

A   international restaurants.
B   historical buildings.
C   arts and crafts.

13 Clothes designed by entrants for the Young Fashion competition must

A   be modelled by the designers themselves.
B   be inspired by aspects of contemporary culture.
C   be made from locally produced materials.

14 Car parking is free in some car parks if you

A   stay for less than an hour.
B   buy something in the shops.
C   park in the evenings or at weekends.

Questions 15–20

Label the map below.

*Write the correct letter, **A–I**, next to Questions 15–20.*

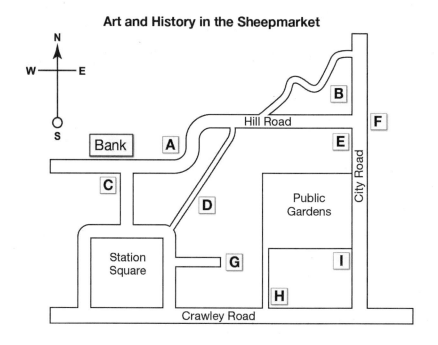

Art and History in the Sheepmarket

15	The Reynolds House	....
16	The Thumb	....
17	The Museum	....
18	The Contemporary Art Gallery	....
19	The Warner Gallery	....
20	Nucleus	....

SECTION 3   *Questions 21–30*

Questions 21–24

Complete the table below.

*Write **ONE WORD ONLY** for each answer.*

Presentation on film adaptations of Shakespeare's plays

Stages of presentation	Work still to be done
Introduce Giannetti's book containing a **21** .... of adaptations	Organise notes
Ask class to suggest the **22** .... adaptations	No further work needed
Present Rachel Malchow's ideas	Prepare some **23** ....
Discuss relationship between adaptations and **24** .... at the time of making the film	No further work needed

Questions 25–30

What do the speakers say about each of the following films?

Choose **SIX** answers from the box and write the correct letter, **A–G**, next to questions 25–30.

<table>
<tr><td colspan="2" align="center">**Comments**</td></tr>
<tr><td>**A**</td><td>clearly shows the historical period</td></tr>
<tr><td>**B**</td><td>contains only parts of the play</td></tr>
<tr><td>**C**</td><td>is too similar to another kind of film</td></tr>
<tr><td>**D**</td><td>turned out to be unpopular with audiences</td></tr>
<tr><td>**E**</td><td>presents the play in a different period from the original</td></tr>
<tr><td>**F**</td><td>sets the original in a different country</td></tr>
<tr><td>**G**</td><td>incorporates a variety of art forms</td></tr>
</table>

Films

25 *Ran*   ....

26 *Much Ado About Nothing*   ....

27 *Romeo & Juliet*   ....

28 *Hamlet*   ....

29 *Prospero's Books*   ....

30 *Looking for Richard*   ....

SECTION 4   *Questions 31–40*

Complete the notes below.

Write **ONE WORD ONLY** *for each answer.*

Noise in Cities

Past research focused on noise level (measured in decibels) and people's responses.

Noise 'maps'

- show that the highest noise levels are usually found on roads
- do not show other sources of noise, e.g. when windows are open or people's neighbours are in their **31** ....
- ignore variations in people's perceptions of noise
- have made people realize that the noise is a **32** .... issue that must be dealt with

Problems caused by noise

- sleep disturbance
- increase in amount of stress
- effect on the **33** .... of schoolchildren

Different types of noise

Some noises can be considered pleasant e.g. the sound of a **34** .... in a town

To investigate this, researchers may use methods from **35** .... sciences e.g. questionnaires

What people want

Plenty of activity in urban environments which are **36** .... , but also allow people to relax

But architects and town planners

- do not get much **37** .... in acoustics
- regard sound as the responsibility of engineers

Understanding sound as an art form

We need to know

- how sound relates to **38** ....
- what can be learnt from psychology about the effects of sound
- whether physics can help us understand the **39** .... of sound

Virtual reality programs

- advantage: predict the effect of buildings
- current disadvantage: they are **40** ....

READING

READING PASSAGE 1

*You should spend about 20 minutes on **Questions 1–13**, which are based on Reading Passage 1 below.*

The History of Glass

From our earliest origins, man has been making use of glass. Historians have discovered that a type of natural glass – obsidian – formed in places such as the mouth of a volcano as a result of the intense heat of an eruption melting sand – was first used as tips for spears. Archaeologists have even found evidence of man-made glass which dates back to 4000 BC; this took the form of glazes used for coating stone beads. It was not until 1500 BC, however, that the first hollow glass container was made by covering a sand core with a layer of molten glass.

Glass blowing became the most common way to make glass containers from the first century BC. The glass made during this time was highly coloured due to the impurities of the raw material. In the first century AD, methods of creating colourless glass were developed, which was then tinted by the addition of colouring materials. The secret of glass making was taken across Europe by the Romans during this century. However, they guarded the skills and technology required to make glass very closely, and it was not until their empire collapsed in 476 AD that glass-making knowledge became widespread throughout Europe and the Middle East. From the 10th century onwards, the Venetians gained a reputation for technical skill and artistic ability in the making of glass bottles, and many of the city's craftsmen left Italy to set up glassworks throughout Europe.

A major milestone in the history of glass occurred with the invention of lead crystal glass by the English glass manufacturer George Ravenscroft (1632–1683). He attempted to counter the effect of clouding that sometimes occurred in blown glass by introducing lead to the raw materials used in the process. The new glass he created was softer and easier to decorate, and had a higher refractive index, adding to its brilliance and beauty, and it proved invaluable to the optical industry. It is thanks to Ravenscroft's invention that optical lenses, astronomical telescopes, microscopes and the like became possible.

In Britain, the modern glass industry only really started to develop after the repeal of the Excise Act in 1845. Before that time, heavy taxes had been placed on the amount of glass melted in a glasshouse, and were levied continuously from 1745 to 1845. Joseph Paxton's Crystal Palace at London's Great Exhibition of 1851 marked the beginning of glass as a material used in the building industry. This revolutionary new building encouraged the use of glass in public, domestic and horticultural architecture. Glass manufacturing techniques also improved with the advancement of science and the development of better technology.

From 1887 onwards, glass making developed from traditional mouth-blowing to a semi-automatic process, after factory-owner HM Ashley introduced a machine capable of producing 200 bottles per hour in Castleford, Yorkshire, England – more than three times quicker than any previous production method. Then in 1907, the first fully automated machine was developed in the USA by Michael Owens – founder of the Owens Bottle Machine Company (later the major manufacturers Owens-Illinois) – and installed in its factory. Owens' invention could produce an impressive 2,500 bottles per hour. Other developments followed rapidly, but it was not until the First World War, when Britain became cut off from essential glass suppliers, that glass became part of the scientific sector. Previous to this, glass had been seen as a craft rather than a precise science.

Today, glass making is big business. It has become a modern, hi-tech industry operating in a fiercely competitive global market where quality, design and service levels are critical to maintaining market share. Modern glass plants are capable of making millions of glass containers a day in many different colours, with green, brown and clear remaining the most popular. Few of us can imagine modern life without glass. It features in almost every aspect of our lives – in our homes, our cars and whenever we sit down to eat or drink. Glass packaging is used for many products, many beverages are sold in glass, as are numerous foodstuffs, as well as medicines and cosmetics.

Glass is an ideal material for recycling, and with growing consumer concern for green issues, glass bottles and jars are becoming ever more popular. Glass recycling is good news for the environment. It saves used glass containers being sent to landfill. As less energy is needed to melt recycled glass than to melt down raw materials, this also saves fuel and production costs. Recycling also reduces the need for raw materials to be quarried, thus saving precious resources.

Questions 1–8

Complete the notes below.

*Choose **ONE WORD ONLY** from the passage for each answer.*

Write your answers in boxes 1–8 on your answer sheet.

The History of Glass

- Early humans used a material called **1** .... to make the sharp points of their **2** ....

- 4000 BC: **3** .... made of stone were covered in a coating of man-made glass.

- First century BC: glass was coloured because of the **4** .... in the material.

- Until 476 AD: Only the **5** .... knew how to make glass.

- From 10th century: Venetians became famous for making bottles out of glass.

- 17th century: George Ravenscroft developed a process using **6** .... to avoid the occurrence of **7** .... in blown glass.

- Mid-19th century: British glass production developed after changes to laws concerning **8** ....

Questions 9–13

In boxes 9–13 on your answer sheet, write

> **TRUE**   *if the statement agrees with the information*
> **FALSE**   *if the statement contradicts the information*
> **NOT GIVEN** *if there is no information on this*

9   In 1887, HM Ashley had the fastest bottle-producing machine that existed at the time.

10   Michael Owens was hired by a large US company to design a fully-automated bottle manufacturing machine for them.

11   Nowadays, most glass is produced by large international manufacturers.

12   Concern for the environment is leading to an increased demand for glass containers.

13   It is more expensive to produce recycled glass than to manufacture new glass.

READING PASSAGE 2

*You should spend about 20 minutes on **Questions 14–26**, which are based on Reading Passage 2 below.*

Bring back the big cats

It's time to start returning vanished native animals to Britain, says John Vesty

There is a poem, written around 598 AD, which describes hunting a mystery animal called a *llewyn*. But what was it? Nothing seemed to fit, until 2006, when an animal bone, dating from around the same period, was found in the Kinsey Cave in northern England. Until this discovery, the lynx – a large spotted cat with tasselled ears – was presumed to have died out in Britain at least 6,000 years ago, before the inhabitants of these islands took up farming. But the 2006 find, together with three others in Yorkshire and Scotland, is compelling evidence that the lynx and the mysterious *llewyn* were in fact one and the same animal. If this is so, it would bring forward the tassel-eared cat's estimated extinction date by roughly 5,000 years.

However, this is not quite the last glimpse of the animal in British culture. A 9th-century stone cross from the Isle of Eigg shows, alongside the deer, boar and aurochs pursued by a mounted hunter, a speckled cat with tasselled ears. Were it not for the animal's backside having worn away with time, we could have been certain, as the lynx's stubby tail is unmistakable. But even without this key feature, it's hard to see what else the creature could have been. The lynx is now becoming the totemic animal of a movement that is transforming British environmentalism: rewilding.

Rewilding means the mass restoration of damaged ecosystems. It involves letting trees return to places that have been denuded, allowing parts of the seabed to recover from trawling and dredging, permitting rivers to flow freely again. Above all, it means bringing back missing species. One of the most striking findings of modern ecology is that ecosystems without large predators behave in completely different ways from those that retain them. Some of them drive dynamic processes that resonate through the whole food chain, creating niches for hundreds of species that might otherwise struggle to survive. The killers turn out to be bringers of life.

Such findings present a big challenge to British conservation, which has often selected arbitrary assemblages of plants and animals and sought, at great effort and expense, to prevent them from changing. It has tried to preserve the living world as if it were a jar of pickles, letting nothing in and nothing out, keeping nature in a state of arrested development. But ecosystems are not merely collections of species; they are also the dynamic and ever-shifting relationships between them. And this dynamism often depends on large predators.

At sea the potential is even greater: by protecting large areas from commercial fishing, we could once more see what 18th-century literature describes: vast shoals of fish being chased by fin and sperm whales, within sight of the English shore. This policy would also greatly boost catches in the surrounding seas; the fishing industry's insistence on scouring every inch of seabed, leaving no breeding reserves, could not be more damaging to its own interests.

Rewilding is a rare example of an environmental movement in which campaigners articulate what they are for rather than only what they are against. One of the reasons why the enthusiasm for rewilding is spreading so quickly in Britain is that it helps to create a more inspiring vision than the green movement's usual promise of 'Follow us and the world will be slightly less awful than it would otherwise have been.'

The lynx presents no threat to human beings: there is no known instance of one preying on people. It is a specialist predator of roe deer, a species that has exploded in Britain in recent decades, holding back, by intensive browsing, attempts to re-establish forests. It will also winkle out sika deer: an exotic species that is almost impossible for human beings to control, as it hides in impenetrable plantations of young trees. The attempt to reintroduce this predator marries well with the aim of bringing forests back to parts of our bare and barren uplands. The lynx requires deep cover, and as such presents little risk to sheep and other livestock, which are supposed, as a condition of farm subsidies, to be kept out of the woods.

On a recent trip to the Cairngorm Mountains, I heard several conservationists suggest that the lynx could be reintroduced there within 20 years. If trees return to the bare hills elsewhere in Britain, the big cats could soon follow. There is nothing extraordinary about these proposals, seen from the perspective of anywhere else in Europe. The lynx has now been reintroduced to the Jura Mountains, the Alps, the Vosges in eastern France and the Harz mountains in Germany, and has re-established itself in many more places. The European population has tripled since 1970 to roughly 10,000. As with wolves, bears, beavers, boar, bison, moose and many other species, the lynx has been able to spread as farming has left the hills and people discover that it is more lucrative to protect charismatic wildlife than to hunt it, as tourists will pay for the chance to see it. Large-scale rewilding is happening almost everywhere – except Britain.

Here, attitudes are just beginning to change. Conservationists are starting to accept that the old preservation-jar model is failing, even on its own terms. Already, projects such as Trees for Life in the Highlands provide a hint of what might be coming. An organisation is being set up that will seek to catalyse the rewilding of land and sea across Britain, its aim being to reintroduce that rarest of species to British ecosystems: hope.

Questions 14–18

*Write the correct letter, **A**, **B**, **C** or **D**, in boxes 14–18 on your answer sheet.*

14   What did the 2006 discovery of the animal bone reveal about the lynx?

    A   Its physical appearance was very distinctive.
    B   Its extinction was linked to the spread of farming.
    C   It vanished from Britain several thousand years ago.
    D   It survived in Britain longer than was previously thought.

15   What point does the writer make about large predators in the third paragraph?

    A   Their presence can increase biodiversity.
    B   They may cause damage to local ecosystems.
    C   Their behaviour can alter according to the environment.
    D   They should be reintroduced only to areas where they were native.

16   What does the writer suggest about British conservation in the fourth paragraph?

    A   It has failed to achieve its aims.
    B   It is beginning to change direction.
    C   It has taken a misguided approach.
    D   It has focused on the most widespread species.

17   Protecting large areas of the sea from commercial fishing would result in

    A   practical benefits for the fishing industry.
    B   some short-term losses to the fishing industry.
    C   widespread opposition from the fishing industry.
    D   certain changes to techniques within the fishing industry.

18   According to the author, what distinguishes rewilding from other environmental campaigns?

    A   Its objective is more achievable.
    B   Its supporters are more articulate.
    C   Its positive message is more appealing.
    D   It is based on sounder scientific principles.

Questions 19–22

Complete the summary using the list of words and phrases A–F below.

Write the correct letter, A–F, in boxes 19–22 on your answer sheet.

Reintroducing the lynx to Britain

There would be many advantages to reintroducing the lynx to Britain. While there is no evidence that the lynx has ever put **19** .... in danger, it would reduce the numbers of certain **20** .... whose populations have increased enormously in recent decades. It would present only a minimal threat to **21** .... , provided these were kept away from lynx habitats. Furthermore, the reintroduction programme would also link efficiently with initiatives to return native **22** .... to certain areas of the country.

A	trees	**B**	endangered species	**C**	hillsides
D	wild animals	**E**	humans	**F**	farm animals

Questions 23–26

Do the following statements agree with the claims of the writer in Reading Passage 2?

In boxes 23–26 on your answer sheet, write

YES   *if the statement agrees with the claims of the writer*
NO   *if the statement contradicts the claims of the writer*
NOT GIVEN *if it is impossible to say what the writer thinks about this*

23 Britain could become the first European country to reintroduce the lynx.

24 The large growth in the European lynx population since 1970 has exceeded conservationists' expectations.

25 Changes in agricultural practices have extended the habitat of the lynx in Europe.

26 It has become apparent that species reintroduction has commercial advantages.

READING PASSAGE 3

*You should spend about 20 minutes on **Questions 27–40**, which are based on Reading Passage 3 on pages 89 and 90.*

Questions 27–33

Reading Passage 3 has seven paragraphs, **A–G**.

Choose the correct heading for each paragraph from the list of headings below.

*Write the correct number, **i–viii**, in boxes 27–33 on your answer sheet.*

List of Headings

i	Disputes over financial arrangements regarding senior managers
ii	The impact on companies of being subjected to close examination
iii	The possible need for fundamental change in every area of business
iv	Many external bodies being held responsible for problems
v	The falling number of board members with broad enough experience
vi	A risk that not all directors take part in solving major problems
vii	Boards not looking far enough ahead
viii	A proposal to change the way the board operates

---

27   Paragraph **A**

28   Paragraph **B**

29   Paragraph **C**

30   Paragraph **D**

31   Paragraph **E**

32   Paragraph **F**

33   Paragraph **G**

UK companies need more effective boards of directors

A   After a number of serious failures of governance (that is, how they are managed at the highest level), companies in Britain, as well as elsewhere, should consider radical changes to their directors' roles. It is clear that the role of a board director today is not an easy one. Following the 2008 financial meltdown, which resulted in a deeper and more prolonged period of economic downturn than anyone expected, the search for explanations in the many post-mortems of the crisis has meant blame has been spread far and wide. Governments, regulators, central banks and auditors have all been in the frame. The role of bank directors and management and their widely publicised failures have been extensively picked over and examined in reports, inquiries and commentaries.

B   The knock-on effect of this scrutiny has been to make the governance of companies in general an issue of intense public debate and has significantly increased the pressures on, and the responsibilities of, directors. At the simplest and most practical level, the time involved in fulfilling the demands of a board directorship has increased significantly, calling into question the effectiveness of the classic model of corporate governance by part-time, independent non-executive directors. Where once a board schedule may have consisted of between eight and ten meetings a year, in many companies the number of events requiring board input and decisions has dramatically risen. Furthermore, the amount of reading and preparation required for each meeting is increasing. Agendas can become overloaded and this can mean the time for constructive debate must necessarily be restricted in favour of getting through the business.

C   Often, board business is devolved to committees in order to cope with the workload, which may be more efficient but can mean that the board as a whole is less involved in fully addressing some of the most important issues. It is not uncommon for the audit committee meeting to last longer than the main board meeting itself. Process may take the place of discussion and be at the expense of real collaboration, so that boxes are ticked rather than issues tackled.

D   A radical solution, which may work for some very large companies whose businesses are extensive and complex, is the professional board, whose members would work up to three or four days a week, supported by their own dedicated staff and advisers. There are obvious risks to this and it would be important to establish clear guidelines for such a board to ensure that it did not step on the toes of management by becoming too engaged in the day-to-day running of the company. Problems of recruitment, remuneration and independence could also arise and this structure would not be appropriate for all companies. However, more professional and better-informed boards would have been particularly appropriate for banks where the executives had access to information that part-time non-executive directors lacked, leaving the latter unable to comprehend or anticipate the 2008 crash.

E   One of the main criticisms of boards and their directors is that they do not focus sufficiently on longer-term matters of strategy, sustainability and governance, but instead concentrate too much on short-term financial metrics. Regulatory requirements and the structure of the market encourage this behaviour. The tyranny of quarterly reporting can distort board decision-making, as directors have to 'make the numbers' every four months to meet the insatiable appetite of the market for more data. This serves to encourage the trading methodology of a certain kind of investor who moves in and out of a stock without engaging in constructive dialogue with the company about strategy or performance, and is simply seeking a short-term financial gain. This effect has been made worse by the changing profile of investors due to the globalisation of capital and the increasing use of automated trading systems. Corporate culture adapts and management teams are largely incentivised to meet financial goals.

F   Compensation for chief executives has become a combat zone where pitched battles between investors, management and board members are fought, often behind closed doors but increasingly frequently in the full glare of press attention. Many would argue that this is in the interest of transparency and good governance as shareholders use their muscle in the area of pay to pressure boards to remove underperforming chief executives. Their powers to vote down executive remuneration policies increased when binding votes came into force. The chair of the remuneration committee can be an exposed and lonely role, as Alison Carnwath, chair of Barclays Bank's remuneration committee, found when she had to resign, having been roundly criticised for trying to defend the enormous bonus to be paid to the chief executive; the irony being that she was widely understood to have spoken out against it in the privacy of the committee.

G   The financial crisis stimulated a debate about the role and purpose of the company and a heightened awareness of corporate ethics. Trust in the corporation has been eroded and academics such as Michael Sandel, in his thoughtful and bestselling book *What Money Can't Buy*, are questioning the morality of capitalism and the market economy. Boards of companies in all sectors will need to widen their perspective to encompass these issues and this may involve a realignment of corporate goals. We live in challenging times.

Questions 34–37

Do the following statements agree with the claims of the writer in Reading Passage 3?

In boxes 34–37 on your answer sheet, write

> **YES**   *if the statement agrees with the claims of the writer*
> **NO**   *if the statement contradicts the claims of the writer*
> **NOT GIVEN**   *if it is impossible to say what the writer thinks about this*

34   Close scrutiny of the behaviour of boards has increased since the economic downturn.

35   Banks have been mismanaged to a greater extent than other businesses.

36   Board meetings normally continue for as long as necessary to debate matters in full.

37   Using a committee structure would ensure that board members are fully informed about significant issues.

Questions 38–40

Complete the sentences below.

*Choose **ONE WORD ONLY** from the passage for each answer.*

Write your answers in boxes 38–40 on your answer sheet.

38   Before 2008, non-executive directors were at a disadvantage because of their lack of ....

39   Boards tend to place too much emphasis on .... considerations that are only of short-term relevance.

40   On certain matters, such as pay, the board may have to accept the views of ....

WRITING

WRITING TASK 1

You should spend about 20 minutes on this task.

The diagram below shows how geothermal energy is used to produce electricity.

Summarise the information by selecting and reporting the main features, and make comparisons where relevant.

Write at least 150 words.

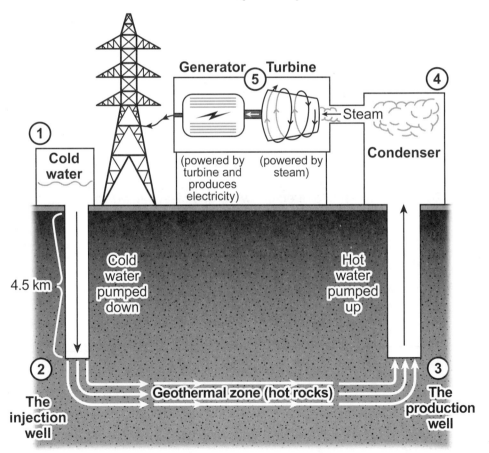

Geothermal power plant

WRITING TASK 2

You should spend about 40 minutes on this task.

Write about the following topic:

> *Some people believe that allowing children to make their own choices on everyday matters (such as food, clothes and entertainment) is likely to result in a society of individuals who only think about their own wishes. Other people believe that it is important for children to make decisions about matters that affect them.*
>
> *Discuss both these views and give your own opinion.*

Give reasons for your answer and include any relevant examples from your own knowledge or experience.

Write at least 250 words.

SPEAKING

PART 1

The examiner asks the candidate about him/herself, his/her home, work or studies and other familiar topics.

EXAMPLE

Art

* Did you enjoy doing art lessons when you were a child? [Why?/Why not?]
* Do you ever draw or paint pictures now? [Why?/Why not?]
* When was the last time you went to an art gallery or exhibition? [Why?]
* What kind of pictures do you like having in your home? [Why?]

PART 2

Describe a time when you visited a friend or family member at their workplace.

You should say:
    who you visited
    where this person worked
    why you visited this person's workplace
and explain how you felt about visiting this person's workplace.

You will have to talk about the topic for one to two minutes. You have one minute to think about what you are going to say. You can make some notes to help you if you wish.

PART 3

Discussion topics:

Different kinds of workplaces

Example questions:
What things make an office comfortable to work in?
Why do some people prefer to work outdoors?
Do you agree that the building people work in is more important than the colleagues they work with?

The importance of work

Example questions:
What would life be like if people didn't have to work?
Are all jobs of equal importance?
Why do some people become workaholics?

Audioscripts

TEST 5

SECTION 1

TC EMPLOYEE: Hi. Can I help you?

VISITOR: I'd like to find out if you have any excursions suitable for families.

TC EMPLOYEE: Sure. How about taking your family for a cruise? We have a steamship that takes passengers out several times a day – it's over 100 years old. *Example*

VISITOR: That sounds interesting. How long is the trip?

TC EMPLOYEE: About an hour and a half. And don't forget to take pictures of the mountains. *Q1* They're all around you when you're on the boat and they look fantastic.

VISITOR: OK. And I assume there's a café or something on board?

TC EMPLOYEE: Sure. How old are your children?

VISITOR: Er, my daughter's fifteen and my son's seven.

TC EMPLOYEE: Right. Well there are various things you can do once you've crossed the lake, to make a day of it. One thing that's very popular is a visit to the Country Farm. You're met off the boat by the farmer and he'll take you to the holding pens, where the sheep are kept. Children love feeding them!

VISITOR: My son would love that. He really likes animals.

TC EMPLOYEE: Well, there's also a 40-minute trek round the farm on a horse, if he wants. *Q2*

VISITOR: Do you think he'd manage it? He hasn't done that before.

TC EMPLOYEE: Sure. It's suitable for complete beginners.

VISITOR: Ah, good.

TC EMPLOYEE: And again, visitors are welcome to explore the farm on their own, as long as they take care to close gates and so on. There are some very beautiful *Q3* gardens along the side of the lake which also belong to the farm – they'll be just at their best now. You could easily spend an hour or two there.

VISITOR: OK. Well that all sounds good. And can we get lunch there? *Q4*

TC EMPLOYEE: You can, and it's very good, though it's not included in the basic cost. You pay when you get there.

VISITOR: Right.

VISITOR: So is there anything else to do over on that side of the lake?

TC EMPLOYEE: Well, what you can do is take a bike over on the ship and then go on a cycling trip. There's a trail there called the Back Road – you could easily spend three or four hours exploring it, and the scenery's wonderful. They'll give you a map *Q5* when you get your ticket for the cruise – there's no extra charge.

VISITOR: What's the trail like in terms of difficulty?

TC EMPLOYEE: Quite challenging in places. It wouldn't be suitable for your seven-year-old. It *Q6* needs someone who's got a bit more experience.

VISITOR: Hmm. Well, my daughter loves cycling and so do I, so maybe the two of us could go, and my wife and son could stay on the farm. That might work out quite well. But we don't have bikes here... is there somewhere we could rent them?

TC EMPLOYEE: Yes, there's a place here in the city. It's called Ratchesons. *Q7*

VISITOR: I'll just make a note of that – er, how do you spell it?

TC EMPLOYEE:	R-A-T-C-H-E-S-O-N-S. It's just by the cruise ship terminal.	
VISITOR:	OK.	
TC EMPLOYEE:	You'd also need to pick up a repair kit for the bike from there to take along with you, and you'd need to take along a snack and some water – it'd be best to get those in the city.	
VISITOR:	Fine. That shouldn't be a problem. <u>And I assume I can rent a helmet from the bike place?</u>	Q8
TC EMPLOYEE:	<u>Sure, you should definitely get that.</u> It's a great ride, but you want to be well prepared because <u>it's very remote – you won't see any shops round there, or anywhere to stay</u>, so you need to get back in time for the last boat.	Q9
VISITOR:	Yeah. So what sort of prices are we looking at here?	
TC EMPLOYEE:	Let's see, that'd be one adult and one child for the cruise with farm tour, that's $117, and an adult and a child for the cruise only so that's $214 dollars altogether. Oh, wait a minute, how old did you say your daughter was?	
VISITOR:	Fifteen.	
TC EMPLOYEE:	Then I'm afraid <u>it's $267</u> because she has to pay the adult fare, which is $75 instead of the child fare which is $22 – sorry about that.	Q10
VISITOR:	That's OK. Er, so how do ...	

SECTION 2

Good morning everyone. My name's Joy Parkins and I'm the restaurant manager. And I understand that none of you've had any previous experience as kitchen assistants? Well, you might be feeling a bit nervous now, but most of our kitchen assistants say they enjoy the work. OK, they might get shouted at sometimes, but it's nothing personal, and <u>they're pleased that they have so many different things to do, which means they never get bored</u>. And I'll tell you straightaway that if you do well, we might think about moving you up and giving you some more responsibility.   Q11

Right, well, you've all shown up on time, which is an excellent start. Now I'm glad to see none of you have unsuitable footwear, so that's good – you need to be careful as the floors can get very wet and slippery. Those of you with long hair have got it well out of the way, <u>but some of you'll need to remove your rings and bracelets – just put them somewhere safe for today, and remember to leave them at home tomorrow, as they can be a safety hazard</u>.   Q12

<u>Now it's going to be a busy day for you all today – we don't have any tables free for this evening, and only a few for lunch.</u> Fortunately we've got our Head Chef back – he was away on holiday all last week which meant the other chefs had extra work. Now, I'll tell you a bit more about the job in a minute but first, some general regulations. For all of you, whatever your age, there's some equipment you mustn't use until you've been properly trained, like the waste disposal system for example, for health and safety reasons. <u>Then I think there are two of you here who are under 18 – that's Emma and Jake, isn't it? Right, so for you two, the meat slicer is out of bounds.</u> And of course none of you are allowed to use the electric mixer until you've been shown how it works.   Q13   Q14

Now you may have heard that this can be a stressful job, and I have to say that can be true. You'll be working an eight-hour day for the first week, though you'll have the chance to do overtime after that as well if you want to. But however long the hours are, you'll get a break in the middle. <u>What you will find is that you're on your feet all day long, lifting and carrying, so if you're not fit now you soon will be! You'll find you don't have much chance to take it easy – when someone tells you to do something you need to do it straightaway</u> – but at least we do have a very efficient air conditioning system compared with some kitchens.   Q15 & Q16

Now let me tell you about some of the people you need to know. So as I said, <u>I'm Joy Parkins</u> <u>and I decide who does what during the day and how long they work for.</u> I'll be trying to get you to work with as many different people in the kitchen as possible, so that you learn while you're on the job. <u>One person whose name you must remember is David Field. If you injure</u> <u>yourself at all, even if it's really minor, you must report to him and he'll make sure the incident</u> <u>is recorded and you get the appropriate treatment.</u> He's trained to give basic treatment to staff himself, or he'll send you off somewhere else if necessary. <u>Then there's Dexter Wills –</u> <u>he's the person you need to see if you smash a plate or something like that.</u> Don't just leave it and hope no one will notice – it's really important to get things noted and replaced or there could be problems later. <u>And finally, there's Mike Smith. He's the member of staff who takes</u> <u>care of all the stores of perishables, so if you notice we're getting low in flour or sugar or</u> <u>something, make sure you let him know so he can put in an order.</u>

Q17

Q18

Q19

Q20

OK, now the next thing …

SECTION 3

TRUDIE: OK, Stewart. We need to start planning our paper on public libraries. Have you thought of an angle yet?

STEWART: Well, there's so much we could look into. How libraries have changed over the centuries, for instance, or how different countries organise them. What do *you* think, Trudie?

TRUDIE: <u>Maybe we should concentrate on this country, and try and relate the changes in</u> <u>libraries to external developments, like the fact that far more people can read than</u> <u>a century ago, and that the local population may speak lots of different languages.</u>

Q21

STEWART: We could include something about changes in the source of funding, too.

TRUDIE: Yes, but remember we're only supposed to write a short paper, so it's probably best if we don't go into funding in any detail.

STEWART: Right. Well, shall we just brainstorm a few ideas, to get started?

TRUDIE: OK. We obviously need to look at the impact of new technology, particularly the internet. Now that lots of books have been digitalised, people can access them from their own computers at home.

STEWART: And if everyone did that, libraries would be obsolete.

TRUDIE: Yes.

STEWART: <u>But the digitalised books that are available online for free are mostly out of</u> <u>copyright, aren't they? And copyright in this country lasts for 70 years after the</u> <u>author dies. So you won't find the latest best-seller or up-to-date information.</u>

Q22

TRUDIE: <u>That's an important point.</u> Anyway, I find it hard to concentrate when I'm reading a long text on a screen. I'd much rather read a physical book. And it takes longer to read on a screen.

STEWART: Oh, I prefer it. I suppose it's just a personal preference.

TRUDIE: Mm. I expect that libraries will go on evolving in the next few years. Some have already become centres where community activities take place, like local clubs meeting there. I think that'll become even more common.

STEWART: I'd like to think so, and that they'll still be serving their traditional function, but I'm not so sure. There are financial implications, after all. <u>What I'm afraid will happen is</u> <u>that books and magazines will all disappear, and there'll just be rows and rows of</u> <u>computers.</u> They won't look anything like the libraries we're used to.

Q23

TRUDIE: · Well, we'll see.

TRUDIE:	I've just had an idea. Why don't we make an in-depth study of our local public library as background to our paper?
STEWART:	Yes, that'd be interesting, and raise all sorts of issues. Let's make a list of possible things we could ask about, then work out some sort of structure. <u>For instance, um, we could interview some of the staff, and find out whether the library has its own budget, or if that's controlled by the local council.</u>
TRUDIE:	And what their policies are. I know they don't allow food, but I'd love to find out what types of noise they ban – there always seems to be a lot of talking, but never music. I don't know if that's a policy or it just happens.
STEWART:	Ah, I've often wondered. <u>Then there are things like how the library is affected by employment laws. I suppose there are rules about working hours, facilities for staff, and so on.</u>
TRUDIE:	Right. <u>Then there are other issues relating to the design of the building and how customers use it. Like what measures does the library take to ensure their safety?</u> They'd need floor coverings that aren't slippery, and emergency exits, for instance. Oh, and another thing – <u>there's the question of the kind of insurance the library needs to have, in case anyone gets injured</u>.
STEWART:	Yes, that's something else to find out. You know something I've often wondered?
TRUDIE:	What's that?
STEWART:	Well, you know they've got an archive of local newspapers going back years? Well, <u>next to it they've got the diary of a well-known politician from the late 19th century.</u> I wonder why it's there. Do you know what his connection was with this area?
TRUDIE:	No idea. Let's add it to our list of things to find out. Oh, I've just thought – <u>you know people might ask in the library about local organisations, like sports clubs? Well, I wonder if they keep a database, or whether they just look online.</u>
STEWART:	Right. <u>I quite fancy finding out what the differences are between a library that's open to the public and one that's part of a museum, for example</u> – they must be very different.
TRUDIE:	Mmm. Then something else I'd like to know is …

Q24

Q25

Q26

Q27

Q28

Q29

Q30

SECTION 4

In public discussion of business, we take certain values for granted. Today I'm going to talk about four of them: collaboration, hard work, creativity and excellence. Most people would say they're all 'good things'. I'm going to suggest that's an over-simple view.

The trouble with these values is that they're theoretical concepts, removed from the reality of day-to-day business. <u>Pursue values by all means, but be prepared for what may happen as a result. They can actually cause damage, which is not at all the intention.</u>   Q31

Business leaders generally try to do the right thing. But <u>all too often the right thing backfires, if those leaders adopt values without understanding and managing the side effects that arise.</u>   Q32 The values can easily get in the way of what's actually intended.

OK. So the first value I'm going to discuss is collaboration. Er, let me give you an example. <u>On a management training course I once attended, we were put into groups and had to construct a bridge across a stream</u>, using building blocks that we were given. The rule was that everyone in the team had to move at least one building block during the construction. This was intended to encourage teamwork.   Q33

But it was really a job best done by one person. <u>The other teams tried to collaborate on</u>   *Q34*
<u>building the structure, and descended into confusion</u>, with everyone getting in each other's
way. Our team leader solved the challenge brilliantly. She simply asked everyone in the team
to move a piece a few centimetres, to comply with the rule, and then let the person in the
team with an aptitude for puzzles like this build it alone. We finished before any other team.
My point is that the task wasn't really suited to teamworking, so why make it one?

Teamwork can also lead to inconsistency – a common cause of poor sales. <u>In the case of</u>   *Q35*
<u>a smartphone that a certain company launched, one director wanted to target the business</u>
<u>market, and another demanded it was aimed at consumers. The company wanted both</u>
<u>directors to be involved, so gave the product a consumer-friendly name, but marketed it to</u>
<u>companies. The result was that it met the needs of neither group. It would have been better</u>
<u>to let one director or the other have his way, not both.</u>

Now industriousness, or hard work. It's easy to mock people who say they work hard: after
all, a hamster running around in a wheel is working hard – and getting nowhere. Of course
<u>hard work is valuable, but only when properly targeted. Otherwise it wastes the resources</u>   *Q36*
<u>that companies value most – time and energy. And that's bad for the organisation.</u>

There's a management model that groups people according to four criteria: clever, hard-
working, stupid and lazy. <u>Here 'lazy' means having a rational determination not to carry out</u>   *Q37*
<u>unnecessary tasks.</u> It doesn't mean trying to avoid work altogether. Most people display two
of these characteristics, and the most valuable people are those who are both clever and
lazy: they possess intellectual clarity, and they don't rush into making decisions. They come
up with solutions to save the time and energy spent by the stupid and hard-working group.
Instead of throwing more man-hours at a problem, the clever and lazy group looks for a more
effective solution.

Next we come to creativity. This often works well – creating an attention-grabbing TV
commercial, for example, might lead to increased sales. But it isn't *always* a good thing.
Some advertising campaigns are remembered for their creativity, without having any effect
on sales. <u>This happened a few years ago with the launch of a chocolate bar: subsequent</u>   *Q38*
<u>research showed that plenty of consumers remembered the adverts, but had no idea what</u>
<u>was being advertised.</u> The trouble is that the creator derives pleasure from coming up with
the idea, and wrongly assumes the audience for the campaign will share that feeling.

A company that brings out thousands of new products may *seem* more creative than a
company that only has a few, but it may be *too* creative, and make smaller profits. <u>Creativity</u>   *Q39*
<u>needs to be targeted, to solve a problem that the company has identified.</u> Just coming up with
more and more novel products isn't necessarily a good thing.

And finally, excellence. We all know companies that claim they 'strive for excellence', but
it takes a long time to achieve excellence. In business, being *first* with a product is more
profitable than having the *best* product. A major study of company performance compared
pioneers – that is, companies bringing out the *first* version of a particular product – with
followers, the companies that copied and improved on that product. <u>The study found that the</u>   *Q40*
<u>pioneers commanded an average market share of 29 percent, while the followers achieved</u>
<u>less than half that, only 13 percent</u> – even though their product might have been better.

Insisting on excellence in everything we do is time-consuming, wastes energy and leads
to losing out on opportunities. Sometimes, second-rate work is more worthwhile than
excellence. 'Make sure it's excellent' *sounds* like a good approach to business, but the 'just-
get-started' approach is likely to be more successful.

TEST 6

SECTION 1

MAN:	Good morning, Kenton Festival box office. How can I help you?
WOMAN:	Oh, good morning. I'm coming to Kenton for a few days' holiday next month, and a friend told me there's a festival. She gave me this number to find out about it.
MAN:	That's right, the festival begins on the 16th of May and goes on till the 19th.

Example

MAN: That's right, <u>the festival begins on the 16th of May</u> and goes on till the 19th.

WOMAN: Oh, that's great. I'll be there from the 15th till the 19th. So could you tell me the programme, please?

MAN: Well, on the first day, there's the opening ceremony, in the town centre. People start gathering around 2 o'clock, to get a good place to see from, and <u>the events will start at 2.45</u>, and finish about 5.30. *Q1*

WOMAN: OK, thanks. I'll make sure I get there early to get a good spot.

MAN: The festival will be officially opened by the mayor. He'll just speak for a few minutes, welcoming everyone to the festival. All the town councillors will be there, and of course lots of other people.

WOMAN: Right.

MAN: <u>Then there'll be a performance by a band.</u> Most years we have a children's choir, but this year the local army cadets offered to perform, and they're very good. *Q2*

WOMAN: Uhuh.

MAN: <u>After that, a community group from the town will perform a play they've written themselves, just a short one. It's about Helen Tungate.</u> I don't know if you've heard of her? *Q3*

WOMAN: I certainly have. <u>She was a scientist years ago.</u> *Q4*

MAN: That's right. She was born in Kenton exactly 100 years ago, so we're celebrating her centenary.

WOMAN: I'm a biologist, so I've always been interested in her. I didn't realise she came from Kenton.

MAN: Yes. Well, all that will take place in the afternoon, and <u>later, as the sun sets, there'll be a firework display. You should go to the park to watch, as you'll get the best view from there, and the display takes place on the opposite side of the river.</u> It's always one of the most popular events in the festival. *Q5*

WOMAN: Sounds great.

WOMAN: And what's happening on the other days?

MAN: There are several events that go on the whole time. For example, <u>the students of the art college have produced a number of videos, all connected with relationships between children and their grandparents.</u> *Q6*

WOMAN: That sounds interesting. It makes a change from children and parents, doesn't it!

MAN: Exactly. Because the art college is in use for classes, throughout the festival, <u>the videos are being shown in Handsworth House.</u> *Q7*

WOMAN: How do you spell the name?

MAN: H-A-N-D-S-W-O-R-T-H. Handsworth House. It's close to the Town Hall.

WOMAN: Right.

MAN: Now let me see, what else can I tell you about?

WOMAN: Are there any displays of ballet dancing? I'm particularly interested in that as I do it as a hobby.

MAN: There isn't any ballet, I'm afraid, but <u>there'll be a demonstration of traditional dances from all round the country.</u> *Q8*

WOMAN:	Oh, that'd be nice. Where's that being held?
MAN:	It's in the market in the town centre – the outdoor one, not the covered market. And
	it's on at 2 and 5 every afternoon of the festival, apart from the first day.
WOMAN:	Lovely. I'm interested in all kinds of dancing, so I'm sure I'll enjoy that!
MAN:	Mmm. I'm sure you will.
WOMAN:	And I'd really like to go to some concerts, if there are any.
MAN:	Yes, there are several. Three performed by professionals, and one by local children.
WOMAN:	And where is it being held?
MAN:	It's in the library, which is in Park Street. On the 18th, at 6.30 in the evening.
WOMAN:	I presume I'll need tickets for that.
MAN:	Yes, you can book online, or you can buy them when you arrive in Kenton, either at
	the festival box office, or from any shops displaying our logo in the windows.
WOMAN:	Well, I think that'll keep me busy for the whole of my stay in Kenton. Thank you so
	much for all your help.
MAN:	You're welcome. I hope you enjoy your stay.
WOMAN:	Thank you. Goodbye.

Q9 (lines 1–2), Q10 (Yes, you can book...)

SECTION 2

Right. I've now almost succeeded in finalising plans for our tour, so I'll bring you up to date with what I know.

As you know, we're flying first to Munich, on Monday the 4th.

The flight is at 11.30, so it's too early to have lunch at the airport. I suggest we meet there for coffee at 10, which should give us plenty of time for breakfast before we leave home. *Q11*

When we arrive in Munich, we'll be met at the airport by Claus Bauer. Claus works for a tour operator, and he'll look after us for the time we'll be in Germany. He's already liaised with the managers of the theatres we're going to visit, and he's also arranged for an officer of the National Theatre in Munich to show us round the theatre one afternoon during our stay. *Q12*

Now last time we discussed this trip, I didn't have the precise cost for hotel rooms, but now I have. The normal rate at the hotel where we're staying is 150 euros a night for a double room. I'd hoped to get that down to 120 euros, but in fact I've been able to negotiate a rate of 110. That'll be reflected in the final payment which you'll need to make by the end of this week. *Q13*

On Tuesday, the day after our arrival, I had hoped we could sit in on a rehearsal at one of the theatres, but unfortunately that's proved very difficult to arrange, so instead we'll have a coach trip to one of the amazing castles in the mountains south of Munich.

On Tuesday evening, we'll all have dinner together in a restaurant near our hotel. From talking to you all about your preferences, it was clear that a typical local restaurant would be too meat-oriented for some of you. Some of you suggested an Italian restaurant, but I must confess that I decided to book a Lebanese one, as we have plenty of opportunities to go to an Italian restaurant at home. *Q14*

On Wednesday afternoon, the director of the play we're going to see that evening will talk to us at the theatre. She'll describe the whole process of producing a play, including how she chose the actors, and, as the play we're going to see is a modern one, how she worked with the playwright. *Q15*

Right. Now I'd just like to make a few points about the plays we're going to see, partly because it might influence your choice of clothes to take with you!

The play we're seeing on Wednesday evening is a modern one, and we're going to the premiere, so it'll be quite a dressy occasion, though of course you don't *have* to dress formally. I gather it's rather a multimedia production, with amazing lighting effects and a soundtrack of electronic music, though unfortunately the playwright is ill and is unlikely to be able to attend.   Q16

On Thursday we're seeing a play that was first performed last year, when it was commissioned to mark a hundred years since the birth in the town of a well-known scientist. We're going to see a revival of that production, which aroused a lot of interest.   Q17

Friday's play will really make you think hard about what clothes to pack, as it'll be in the garden of a palace. It's a beautiful setting, but I'd better warn you, there won't be much protection from the wind.   Q18

On Saturday, we're going by coach to a theatre in another town, not far from Munich. This will   Q19
be the opening of a drama festival, and the mayor and all the other dignitaries of the town will be attending. After the performance, the mayor is hosting a reception for all the audience, and there'll be a band playing traditional music of the region.

And after having a day off on Sunday, our final play is on Monday, and it's in the stunning setting of the old Town Hall, which dates back to the 14th century. The performance marks the fifty years that the lead actor has been on stage, and the play is the one where he made his first professional appearance, all those years ago.   Q20

And the day after that, we'll be flying back home. Now have you got any questions before I …

SECTION 3

BETH: Oh good morning. You must be James. I'm Beth Cartwright – please call me Beth.
JAMES: Thank you.
BETH: Now as this is your first tutorial since you started on the Scandinavian Studies course, I'd like to find out something about you. Why did you decide to take this course?
JAMES: Well, my mother is Danish, and although we always lived in England, she used to   Q21
        talk about her home a lot, and that made me want to visit Denmark. We hardly ever did, though – my mother usually went on her own. But whenever her relations or friends were in England they always came to see us.
BETH: I see. So I assume you already speak Danish, one of the languages you'll be studying.
JAMES: I can get by when I talk to people, though I'm not terribly accurate.
BETH: Now you probably know that you'll spend the third year of the course abroad. Have you had any thoughts about that?
JAMES: I'm really looking forward to it. And although Denmark seems the obvious place to go, because of my family connections, I'd love to spend the time in Iceland.
BETH: Oh, I'm sure it can be arranged. Do you have any plans for when you graduate? A lot of students go on to take a master's degree.
JAMES: I think the four years of the undergraduate course will be enough for me. I'm   Q22
        interested in journalism, and I quite like the idea of moving to Scandinavia and writing for magazines. I'd find that more creative than translating, which I suppose most graduates do.

BETH:	OK. Now how are you finding the courses you're taking this term, James?	
JAMES:	Well, I'm really enjoying the one on Swedish cinema.	
BETH:	<u>That'll continue next term, but the one on Scandinavian literature that's running at the</u> <u>moment will be replaced by more specialised courses.</u> Oh, and by the way, if you're interested in watching Danish television programmes – there's going to be a course on that the term after next.	*Q23*
JAMES:	That sounds good.	
BETH:	Have you started thinking about the literature paper that you have to write in the next few weeks?	
JAMES:	Yes, my first choice would be to do something on the Icelandic sagas.	
BETH:	Hmm. The trouble with that is that a lot of people choose that topic, and it can be difficult to get hold of the books you'll need. Why not leave that for another time?	
JAMES:	Right.	
BETH:	<u>You might find modern novels or 19th century playwrights interesting.</u>	*Q24*
JAMES:	<u>I've read or seen several plays in translation, so that would be a good idea.</u>	
BETH:	Fine. I'll put you down for that topic.	
JAMES:	Right. So what would you advise me to aim at in the paper?	
BETH:	First I suggest you avoid taking one writer and going into a great deal of detail. That approach certainly has its place, but <u>I think you first need to get an understanding</u> <u>of the literature in the context of the society in which it was produced – who it was</u> <u>written for, how it was published, and so on</u>. I also think that's more fruitful than placing it within the history of the genre.	*Q25*
JAMES:	OK, that sounds reasonable.	

JAMES:	Could I ask for some advice about writing the paper I'm working on about the Vikings? I have to do that this week, and I'm a bit stuck.	
BETH:	Of course. Have you decided yet what to write about?	
JAMES:	No, I haven't. There's so much that seems interesting – Viking settlement in other countries, trade, mythology…	
BETH:	Well, <u>what I suggest is that you read an assignment a student wrote last year</u>, which is kept in the library. It's short and well focused, and I'm sure you'll find it helpful. I'll give you the details in a moment. Textbooks usually cover so many topics, it can be very difficult to choose just one.	*Q26*
JAMES:	OK. I've got a DVD of the film about the Vikings that came out earlier this year. Should I watch that again?	
BETH:	If it's the one I am thinking of, hmm, I'd ignore it – it's more fantasy than reality. But <u>I've got a recording of a documentary that you should watch</u>. It makes some interesting and provocative points, which I think will help you to focus your topic.	*Q27*
JAMES:	Right.	
JAMES:	<u>So then should I work out an outline?</u>	*Q28*
BETH:	<u>Yes. Just headings for different sections, at this stage.</u> And <u>then you should start</u> <u>looking for suitable articles and books to draw on, and take notes</u> which you organise according to those headings.	*Q29*
JAMES:	I see.	
BETH:	<u>Then put short phrases and sentences as bullet points under each heading.</u> Make sure that this skeleton makes sense and flows properly, before writing up the paper in full.	*Q30*
JAMES:	OK. Thanks, that's very helpful.	

SECTION 4

Over the years, attitudes towards workers have changed considerably. After all, there was a time when workers had no rights at all, and laboured in appalling conditions. Conditions have improved a lot, but conflict in the workplace is still common. And human resources managers nowadays need to be able to deal with it when necessary.

What is conflict in the workplace? Definitions vary, but I'm taking it to refer to a whole range   Q31
of behaviours that the victim finds unacceptable, from minor, harmless arguments to – at the
opposite extreme – physical violence. Much of this is covered by the term bullying, by which
I mean one or more people behaving abusively or aggressively against another who is in a
weaker position. Although all behaviour like this is a form of conflict, not all conflict can be
described in these terms.

As with all human behaviour, there are numerous reasons for it. But often it's caused by   Q32
someone who feels the need to show their superiority over someone else, in order to feel that
they aren't at the lowest level in a hierarchy or a group of people.

In some cases one person simply dislikes the other, on the basis that the personality of one   Q33
is in some way incompatible with that of the other person. A general habit of optimism in one
person could make them intolerant of a colleague who's constantly pessimistic – not that that
justifies treating them badly, of course.

Some conflicts arise when people are more interested in promoting themselves and their   Q34
team than in the company as a whole. These conflicts are called 'structural', and could come
about, for example, when a sales team believe they are the only people in the business who
do any useful work, and look down on behind-the-scenes administrators.

Conflict obviously affects the individuals concerned – the situation is likely to be very stressful Q35
for victims, resulting in their absence from work, possibly for months. For the company, if no
effort is made to deal with conflict, it can spiral out of control, and even lead to the breakdown
of the business.

Some interesting work with chief executives – CEOs – has uncovered some of the reasons
why they may treat colleagues badly. Many CEOs combine two opposing characteristics: Q36
confidence – that is, the belief that they're capable of great achievements – with a high level
of anxiety, a fear of missing targets, whether set by themselves or by the directors of the
company. This combination can make them respond badly to anyone who questions their
decisions.

In a high pressure work environment, such characteristics become problematic. And it's   Q37
particularly difficult to tackle the situation where colleagues, managers and board members
are all trying to achieve their own visions. When they can't agree on strategic issues and on
where they see the business going, there are real problems.

For managers at lower levels within the organisation, it might seem that an autocratic form
of management – where the chief executive gives orders and everyone else has to obey –
would see more conflict than others. Interestingly, though, a company with a more democratic Q38
business model, can suffer *more*, when uncertainty about who to report to leads to conflicting
demands.

Now I'll say a little about dealing with the type of conflict that has harmful effects. Of course
the ideal is to prevent it arising in the first place. A good manager, at any level, will make   Q39
efforts to earn the respect of the people they work with, particularly those who report to them.
That will involve politeness in all communications, and treating them as equals who happen
to have a different role within the organisation.

Sometimes, of course, conflict does occur, and can get out of hand. In such cases the human resources department often gets involved. However, <u>if one of the parties in a conflict sees human resources as simply a mouthpiece for the chief executive, then an external mediator might be able to help</u>. By talking to both sides, and trying to find the truth of what's been happening, they can build a clear picture of the situation, and give feedback that both sides will accept, precisely *because* they're independent.

Q40

TEST 7

SECTION 1

SUSIE:	Hello?
PAUL:	Hi, Susie, it's Paul here. How are you? Enjoying your new job? You're working at the library, aren't you?
SUSIE:	Yes. I started when <u>the library re-opened a month ago</u>. It's great.
PAUL:	Actually Carol and I have been meaning to join for a while.
SUSIE:	Oh, you should. It doesn't cost anything, and the new library has all sorts of facilities. It's not just a place where you borrow books. For instance, there's an area with comfortable seats where you can sit and read the magazines they have there. Some people spend the whole morning there.
PAUL:	Mmm. Wish I had that amount of time to spend!
SUSIE:	Yes, you must be pretty busy at present, with the children and everything?
PAUL:	We are, yes. But we're hoping to get away this summer. We're thinking of going to Greece.
SUSIE:	Well, <u>we've got a much larger section of the library devoted to travel books now</u>, so you should come and have a look. I can't remember if there's anything specifically on Greece, but I should think so.
PAUL:	OK. Now Carol's organising a project for the history class she teaches at school – it's about life in the town a hundred years ago. Do you have anything that might be useful?
SUSIE:	Yes, actually <u>we've now got a new section with materials on the history of the town and surrounding region</u>.
PAUL:	Right. I'll tell her. You can't always find that sort of thing on the internet. Now in the old library there used to be a separate room with reference books. It was a really nice quiet room.
SUSIE:	Yes. We've put those books in the main part of the library now, but <u>we do have a room called the community room. It can be hired out for meetings, but at other times people can use it to study</u>.
PAUL:	I might use that. It's hard to find anywhere quiet at home sometimes.
SUSIE:	I can't remember how old your son and daughter are … <u>we've introduced a special section of fiction written specially for teenagers</u>, but they might be a bit young for that?
PAUL:	Yes, they would be.

Example

Q1

Q2

Q3

Q4

SUSIE:	Well, we do have lots of activities for younger children.
PAUL:	Yes?
SUSIE:	For example <u>we have a Science Club. At the next meeting, they're going to be doing experiments with stuff that everyone has in the kitchen</u> – sugar and flour and so on.

Q5

PAUL:	They might be interested, yes.	
SUSIE:	And we have a competition for children called Reading Challenge. That doesn't begin until after the end of term. They have to read six books, and they get a certificate if they manage it.	
PAUL:	So that gives them something to do while they're on holiday, instead of getting bored.	
SUSIE:	That's the idea. And there's special activities for adults too. <u>On Friday we have a local author called Tanya Streep who's going to be talking about her new novel. It's called 'Catch the Mouse' and she based the story on a crime that actually took place here years ago.</u>	*Q6*
PAUL:	Right. We're not free on Friday, but I'll look out for the book.	
SUSIE:	Now this probably isn't for you, but <u>we do have IT support available for members. We get quite a few older people coming along who are wanting to get up to speed with computer technology. It's on Tuesday mornings – they don't need to make an appointment or anything, they just turn up.</u>	*Q7*
PAUL:	Well, my mother might be interested, I'll let her know.	
SUSIE:	OK. <u>And there's another service which you wouldn't expect from a library, which is a free medical check-up. The hospital arranges for someone to come along and measure the level of sugar in your blood, and they check cholesterol levels at the same time.</u>	*Q8*
PAUL:	<u>Really</u>?	
SUSIE:	<u>Yes, but that's only for the over-60s</u>, so you wouldn't qualify.	
PAUL:	OK. Well, I'll tell my mother, she might be interested.	
SUSIE:	What other information … well, <u>we do have a little shop with things like wallcharts and greetings cards, and also stamps</u> so you can post the cards straightaway, which is really useful.	*Q9*
PAUL:	Yeah. Well, I'll bring the children round at the weekend and we'll join. Oh, one more thing – I'll be bringing the car, <u>is there parking available?</u>	*Q10*
SUSIE:	<u>Yes, and it's free in the evening and at weekends.</u>	
PAUL:	Perfect. Well, thanks, Susie see you …	

SECTION 2

In this session in your training day we're going to look at some of the more specialised holidays we offer at BC Travel. Now, the travel business is very competitive and it's important to be aware of how the market's changing and developing. In terms of age groups, <u>the over-65s are an important market, and one that's increasing steadily year on year.</u> The fewest holidays are taken by the 31 to 42-year-olds, and that figure shows no sign of rising. The biggest market at present is still the youngest group, the 16 to 30s, but this group's also seen the biggest drop over the last few years, <u>whereas there's a noticeable growth in the number of holidays taken by the 55 to 64-year-olds.</u> As far as the 43 to 54-year-olds are concerned, bookings there are steady, but I have to say we haven't seen the increase we expected. *Q11 & Q12*

One trend we're noticing with nearly all age groups is the growing popularity of holidays in which clients do some kind of specialised activity. I'm not talking here about adventure holidays, where clients take part in high-risk activities like white water rafting just for the thrill of it. Activity holidays usually involve rather less high-risk sports, or things like art and music. They're not necessarily cheaper than ordinary holidays, often the opposite, in fact. But <u>they do often take place outside the main tourist centres, which gives an opportunity for clients to find out more about the local people and customs</u>, and many say this is one of the most positive features of these holidays. Of course, they offer the chance to develop a new skill or *Q13 & Q14* talent, <u>but clients often say that more than this, it's the chance to create lasting relationships</u> <u>with other like-minded people that's the main draw.</u>   *Q13 &* *Q14*

Let me give you some examples of BC Travel activity holidays. Our painting holidays take place in four different centres in France and Italy and they're very popular with clients of all abilities from beginners onwards. <u>We've got an excellent team of artists to lead the classes –</u>   *Q15* <u>some of them have been with us from the start, and five additional ones will be joining us this</u> <u>year</u> so that we can offer a greater number of classes in each centre.

As far as cooking holidays are concerned, I know a <u>lot of agents offer holidays where clients</u>   *Q16* <u>cook recipes related to one particular country, usually the one they're staying in, but we focus</u> <u>on dishes from a great many different ones</u>. Apart from that you'll find the usual emphasis on good quality, organic ingredients – that's more or less a given nowadays – and there are generally some meat-free recipes included.

Our photography holidays take place in a wide range of countries from Iceland to Vietnam, and clients have the opportunity to see some stunning scenery. Groups are small, no more than eight, so <u>clients can have one-on-one tuition during the holiday</u>, and excursions are   *Q17* arranged with fully-trained guides. At the end of each holiday an exhibition is held of the photographs taken so that clients can see one another's work and receive valuable feedback from the tutor.

Finally, let me tell you about our fitness holidays. In Ireland and Italy we run one-week general fitness classes for all ages and levels of fitness. Clients start the course with a consultation with a trainer, and together they draw up an individual programme. As well as improving general fitness, <u>clients find that they end up losing much of the stress they've built</u>   *Q18* <u>up in their daily lives.</u>

<u>In Greece, we have a two-week holiday for clients who want to do something about their</u>   *Q19* <u>weight.</u> This has all the features you'd expect, like a personalised diet programme, but one of its most popular features is that the exercise classes are all held on the beach. People say it's far preferable to being in a gym.

Finally, we offer several holidays in Morocco. One very popular one is the mountain biking holiday. Bikes are provided and there are different routes according to people's ability. <u>We</u>   *Q20* <u>offer one which is tailored to the needs of families</u>, which is particularly popular.

OK, so that's about all the time I have today, so thank you very much ...

SECTION 3

NATALIE: Dave, I'm worried about our case study. I've done a bit of reading, but I'm not sure what's involved in actually writing a case study – I missed the lecture where Dr Baker talked us through it.

DAVE: OK, well it's quite straightforward. We've got our focus – that's tourism at the Horton Castle site. And you said you'd done some reading about it.

NATALIE: Yes, I found some articles and made notes of the main points.

DAVE: <u>Did you remember to keep a record of where you got the information from?</u>   *Q21*

NATALIE: Sure. I know what a pain it is when you forget that.

DAVE: OK, so we can compare what we've read. Then we have to decide on a particular problem or need at our site. And then think about who we're going to interview to get more information.

NATALIE: OK. So who'd that be? <u>The people who work there?</u> And presumably some of the tourists too?   *Q22*

DAVE: Yes, both those groups. So we'll have to go to the site to do that, I suppose. But we might also do some of our interviewing away from the site – <u>we could even contact some people here in the city, like administrators involved in overseeing tourism.</u>   *Q23*

NATALIE: OK. So we'll need to think about our interview questions and fix times and places for the meetings. It's all going to take a lot of time.

DAVE: Mmm. And if we can, we should ask our interviewees if they can bring along some numerical data that we can add to support our findings.

NATALIE: And photographs?

DAVE: I think we have plenty of those already. <u>But Dr Baker also said we have to establish with our interviewees whether we can identify them in our case study, or whether they want to be anonymous.</u>   *Q24*

NATALIE: Oh, I wouldn't have thought of that. OK, once we've got all this information, I suppose we have to analyse it.

DAVE: Yes, put it all together and choose what's relevant to the problem we're focusing on, and <u>analyse that carefully to find out if we can identify any trends or regularities</u> there. That's the main thing at this stage, rather than concentrating on details or lots of facts.   *Q25*

NATALIE: OK. And then once we've analysed that, what next?

DAVE: Well, then we need to think about what we do with the data we've selected to make it as clear as possible to our readers. Things like graphs, or tables, or charts…

NATALIE: Right.

DAVE: Then the case study itself is mostly quite standard; we begin by presenting the problem, and giving some background, then go through the main sections, but the thing that surprised me is that <u>in a normal report we'd end with some suggestions to deal with the problem or need we identified, but in a case study we end up with a question or a series of questions to our readers, and they decide what ought to be done</u>.   *Q26*

NATALIE: Oh, I hadn't realised that.

NATALIE: So basically, the problem we're addressing in our case study of the Horton Castle site is why so few tourists are visiting it. And we'll find out more from our interviews, but I did find one report on the internet that suggested that one reason might be because as far as transport goes, access is difficult.

DAVE: I read that too, but that report was actually written ten years ago, when the road there was really bad, but that's been improved now. And <u>I think there's plenty of fascinating stuff there for a really good day out, but you'd never realise it from the castle website – maybe that's the problem.</u>   *Q27*

NATALIE: <u>Yes, it's really dry and boring.</u>

DAVE: I read somewhere a suggestion that what the castle needs is a visitor centre. So we could have a look for some information about that on the internet. What would we need to know?

NATALIE: Well, who'd use it for a start. It'd be good to know what categories the visitors fell into too, like school parties or retired people, but I think we'd have to talk to staff to get that information.

DAVE: OK. And as we're thinking of suggesting a visitor centre we'd also have to look at potential problems. I mean, obviously it wouldn't be cheap to set up.

NATALIE: No, but it could be a really good investment. <u>And as it's on a historical site it'd need to get special planning permission, I expect. That might be hard.</u>   *Q28*

DAVE: Right, especially as the only possible place for it would be at the entrance, and that's right in front of the castle.

NATALIE: Mmm.

DAVE: But it could be a good thing for the town of Horton. At present it's a bit of a ghost town. <u>Once they've left school and got any skills or qualifications, the young people all get out as fast as they can to get jobs in the city, and the only people left are children and those who've retired.</u> *Q29*

NATALIE: Right. Something else we could investigate would be the potential damage that tourists might cause to the castle site, I mean their environmental impact. At present the tourists can just wander round wherever they want, but <u>if numbers increase, there might have to be some restrictions, like sticking to marked ways. And there'd need to be guides and wardens around to make sure these were enforced.</u> *Q30*

DAVE: Yes, we could look at that too. OK, well …

SECTION 4

OK, so we've been looking at how man-made changes in our environment can affect wildlife. Now I'll discuss a particular example. Let's take a look at mercury. Mercury's one of the 120 or so elements that make up all matter, and it has the symbol Hg. It's a shiny, silvery substance. You may have seen it in old-fashioned thermometers, but it's not used much for domestic purposes now because it's highly toxic.

But the problem is that the amount of mercury in the environment's increasing. The main reason for this is the power plants used to produce electricity. The main source of energy that most of them use is still coal, and when it's burned it releases mercury into the atmosphere. Some of this gets deposited into lakes and rivers, and if it's ingested by a fish it's not excreted, it stays in the fish's body and it enters the food chain. So it's been known for some time that birds which eat fish may be affected, but <u>what wasn't known until quite recently is that those that eat insects can also be affected.</u> *Q31*

So a woman called Claire Varian-Ramos is doing some research on how this is affecting birds.

And rather than looking at how many birds are actually killed by mercury poisoning, she's looking for more subtle sub-effects. And <u>these may be to do with the behaviour of the birds, or with the effect of mercury on the way their brain works, so whether it leads to problems with memory, for example.</u> And she's particularly focusing on the effects of mercury on bird song. <u>Now, the process of song learning happens at a particular stage in the birds' development, and what you may not know is that a young bird seems to acquire this skill by listening to the songs produced by its father</u>, rather than by any other bird. *Q32 Q33*

And Varian-Ramos has already found in her research that <u>if young male birds are exposed to mercury, if they eat food contaminated with mercury, then the songs they produce aren't as complex as those produced by other birds.</u> So quite low-level exposure to mercury is likely to have an impact on male birds in a natural situation, because it can mean that they're less attractive to female birds, and so <u>it can affect their chances of reproduction.</u> *Q34 Q35*

Now the way she's carrying out this research is worth thinking about. She's using a mixture of studies using birds kept in laboratories, and studies carried out outdoors in the wild. <u>The lab-based studies have the advantage that you don't get all the variables you would in a natural setting, so the experimenter has a much higher level of control</u>, and that means they can be more confident about their results in some ways. And of course they don't have to worry about going out and finding the birds in order to observe them. *Q36*

So what are the implications here for humans? Well, <u>because many birds are migratory, they</u>   *Q37*
<u>may be transporting mercury far from contaminated sites. For example, it's been found that</u>
<u>ducks who'd been feeding at a contaminated site were later shot by hunters over a thousand</u>
<u>kilometres away, and presumably eaten.</u> But these birds likely had mercury levels high
enough to warrant concern for human consumption.

In addition, going back to song learning by birds, we saw that this may be affected by
mercury contamination. Well, <u>we also know that in humans, mercury causes developmental</u>   *Q38*
<u>delays in the acquisition of language</u>, and in fact this process is very similar in the brain
regions it involves and even the genes that are involved. But mercury contamination has
other important implications for humans as well. <u>It's now known that an unborn child can be</u>   *Q39*
<u>affected if the food eaten by its mother contains high levels of mercury</u>, and these effects can
be quite substantial.

In the end, it comes down to whether more value is placed on human economic wellbeing
or environmental wellbeing. <u>It's true there are new regulations for mercury emissions from</u>   *Q40*
<u>power plants, but these will need billions of dollars to implement, and increase costs for</u>
<u>everyone.</u> Some argue that's too much to pay to protect wildlife. But as we've seen, the
issues go beyond that, and I think it's an issue we need to consider very carefully.

TEST 8

SECTION 1

BOB:	Hello, Pembroke Cycling Holidays, Bob speaking.
MARGARET:	Oh hello. I've seen your advert for people to lead cycle trips. Are you the right person to speak to?
BOB:	Yes, I am. Could I have your name, please?
MARGARET:	<u>It's Margaret Smith.</u>
BOB:	<u>Are you looking for a permanent job, Margaret?</u>
MARGARET:	<u>No, temporary.</u> I've got a permanent job starting in a few months' time, and I want to do something else until then.
BOB:	What work do you do?
MARGARET:	This will probably sound crazy – I used to be a lawyer, and then I made a complete career change and <u>I'm going to be a doctor</u>. I've just finished my training.
BOB:	Right. And have you had any experience of leading cycle trips?
MARGARET:	Yes, <u>I've led several bike tours in Africa</u>. The trip to India that I had arranged to lead next month has now been cancelled, so when I saw you were advertising for tour leaders, I decided to apply.
BOB:	OK. Now we normally have two or three leaders on a trip, depending on the size of the group. Some tours are for very experienced cyclists, but we've got a tour coming up soon in Spain, which is proving so popular we need an additional leader. It's a cycling holiday for families. Would that suit you?
MARGARET:	It certainly would. I enjoy working with children, and I probably need some more experience before I go on a really challenging trip.
BOB:	That tour includes several teenagers: have you worked with that age group before?
MARGARET:	Yes, <u>I'm a volunteer worker in a youth club</u>, where I help people to improve their cycling skills. Before that I helped out in a cycling club where I taught beginners.

Right-column labels:
Example
Q1

Q2

Q3

Q4

BOB:	Well that's great. Now the trip I mentioned is just for a fortnight, but there might be the possibility of leading other tours after that. Would that fit in with your plans?	
MARGARET:	That'd be fine. <u>I'll be free for five months. My job is due to start on October the 2nd, and I'm available from May the 1st until late September.</u>	*Q5*
BOB:	Good. Now is there anything I need to know about the food you eat? We usually have one or two people in the group who don't eat meat, or have some sort of food allergy, so we're always very careful about that.	
MARGARET:	Yes, <u>I'm allergic to cheese.</u> Would that be a problem?	*Q6*
BOB:	No, as long as we have enough notice, we can deal with that.	
MARGARET:	That's great.	

MARGARET:	It sounds really interesting – would you like me to fill in an application form?	
BOB:	Yes, please. Where should I post it to?	
MARGARET:	Could you send it to <u>27 Arbuthnot Place – A-R-B-U-T-H-N-O-T – Place, Dumfries.</u>	*Q7*
BOB:	<u>And what's the postcode, please</u>?	*Q8*
MARGARET:	<u>DG7 4PH.</u>	
BOB:	Was that P Papa or B Bravo?	
MARGARET:	P Papa.	
BOB:	Got that. If you could return the application form by Friday this week, <u>we can interview you on Tuesday next week.</u> Say half past two. Would that be possible for you?	*Q9*
MARGARET:	Yes, it's fine. You're quite a long way from where I live, so I'll drive over on Monday. Should I bring anything to the interview?	
BOB:	We'll have your application form, of course, but we'll need to see any certificates you've got that are relevant, in cycling, first aid, or whatever.	
MARGARET:	OK.	
BOB:	<u>And at the interview we'd like to find out about your experience of being a tour guide, so could you prepare a ten-minute talk about that, please?</u> You don't need slides or any complicated equipment – just some notes.	*Q10*
MARGARET:	Right. I'll start thinking about that straightaway!	
BOB:	Good. Well, we'll look forward to receiving your application form, and we'll contact you to confirm the interview.	
MARGARET:	Thanks very much.	
BOB:	Thank you, Margaret. Goodbye.	
MARGARET:	Bye.	

SECTION 2

Welcome to this podcast about the Sheepmarket, which is one of the oldest parts of the city. As its name suggests, there was originally a market here where farmers brought their sheep, but now it's been redeveloped into a buzzing, vibrant area of the city, which is also home to one of the city's fastest-growing communities. The nearby university has always meant the area's popular with students, who come in to enjoy the lively nightlife, but <u>now graduates embarking on careers in the worlds of fashion and design are buying up the new apartments recently built here to replace the small houses where the market workers used to live.</u>   *Q11*

<u>The narrow old side streets are great places for finding original pictures, jewellery and ceramics</u> which won't break the bank, as well as local produce like fruit and vegetables. There's also lots of pavement cafes where you can have a coffee and watch tourists from all   *Q12*

over the world go by. The oldest buildings in the area are on the main streets, including the city's first department store, built in the 1880s, which is still open today.

The Sheepmarket is a centre for fashion, and there's a policy of encouraging new young designers. The Young Fashion competition is open to local young people who are passionate about fashion. <u>This year they've been asked to design an outfit based on ideas from the music and technology that's part of their everyday life</u>, using both natural and man-made fibres. The garments will be judged by a panel of experts and fashion designers, and the winning entries will be modelled at a special gala evening.

Q13

Parking at the Sheepmarket is easy. There are plenty of pay and display car parking spaces on the roadsides which are fine if you just want to stay for an hour or two, but if you want to spend the day there it's better to park in one of the four underground car parks. It's not expensive and <u>if you can present a receipt from one of the local stores, you'll not be charged at all</u>. After six pm many of the car parks have a flat rate which varies but it is usually very reasonable.

Q14

The Sheepmarket is one of the main centres for art and history in the whole of the country. If you look at our map, you'll see some of the main attractions there. Most visitors start from Crawley Road, at the bottom of the map. <u>The Reynolds House is one of the oldest houses in the city, and is open to the public. It's on the north side of Crawley Road, next to the footpath that leads to the public gardens.</u>

Q15

The area's particularly interesting for its unusual sculptures. <u>'The Thumb' is just what its name suggests, but it's about 10 metres high. You'll see it on Hill Road, across the road from the Bank.</u>

Q16

<u>The Museum's got a particularly fine collection of New Zealand landscapes. It's on the east side of the Sheepmarket, on City Road. It's on the other side of the road from the public gardens, immediately facing the junction with Hill Road.</u>

Q17

<u>The Contemporary Art Gallery is on a little road that leads off Station Square, not far from the public gardens. The road ends at the gallery – it doesn't go anywhere else.</u> That's open every day except Mondays.

Q18

<u>The Warner Gallery specialises in 19th-century art. It's on City Road, near the junction with Crawley Road, on the same side of the road as the public gardens.</u> It's open on weekdays from 9 to 5, and entry is free.

Q19

<u>Finally, if you're interested in purchasing high quality artwork, the place to go is Nucleus. You need to go from Crawley Road up through Station Square and east along Hill Road until you get to a small winding road turning off. Go up there and it's on your right – if you get to City Road you've gone too far.</u>

Q20

SECTION 3

KATIE: Joe, you know I'm giving a presentation in our film studies class next week?
JOE: Yes.
KATIE: Well, could we discuss it? I could do with getting someone else's opinion.
JOE: Of course, Katie. What are you going to talk about?
KATIE: It's about film adaptations of Shakespeare's plays. I've got very interested in all the different approaches that film directors take.
JOE: Uhuh.

KATIE: So I thought I'd start with Giannetti, who's a professor of film and literature, and in one   *Q21*
of his books he came up with a straightforward classification of film adaptations based
on how faithful they are to the original plays and novels.

JOE: Right.

KATIE: I've already made some notes on that, so I just need to sort those out before the
presentation. I thought that next I'd ask the class to come up with the worst examples   *Q22*
of Shakespeare adaptations that they've seen, and to say why. That should be more
fun than having their favourite versions.

JOE: Yes, I can certainly think of a couple!

KATIE: Right. Next I want to talk about Rachel Malchow. I came across something on the
internet about her work on film adaptations, and I was thinking of showing some film
clips to illustrate her ideas.

JOE: Will you have enough time, though? Both to prepare and during the presentation?
After all, I doubt if you'll be able to find all the clips you want.

KATIE: Hmm. Perhaps you're right. OK, well, I'd better do some slides instead, saying how   *Q23*
various films relate to what she says. That should encourage discussion.

JOE: Mmm.

KATIE: Next I want to say something about how plays may be chosen for adaptation because   *Q24*
they're concerned with issues of the time when the film is made.

JOE: You mean things like patriotism, or the role of governments?

KATIE: Exactly. It's quite tricky, but I've got a few ideas I'd like to discuss.

KATIE: And finally I want to talk about a few adaptations that I think illustrate a range of
approaches, and make some comments on them. Do you know the Japanese film
Ran?

JOE: I haven't seen it. It was based on Shakespeare's *King Lear*, wasn't it?

KATIE: That's right. It was a very loose adaptation, using the same situation and story, but   *Q25*
moving it to 16th century Japan instead of 16th century Britain. So for example the
king's daughters become sons, because in Japanese culture at that time, women
couldn't succeed to the throne.

JOE: OK. I hope you're going to talk about the 1993 film of *Much Ado About Nothing*. I think
that's one of the best Shakespeare films. It really brings the play to life, doesn't it?

KATIE: Yes, I agree. And I think filming it in Italy, where the play is set, makes you see what   *Q26*
life was like at the time of the play.

JOE: Absolutely. Right, what's next?

KATIE: Er, next, I thought *Romeo & Juliet*, the 1996 film, which moves the action into the   *Q27*
present day.

JOE: Yes, it worked really well, I thought – changing the two feuding families in the original
to two competing business empires, even though they're speaking in the English of the
original play.

KATIE: You'd expect it would sound really bizarre, but I found I soon got used to it.

JOE: Me too.

KATIE: Then I thought I'd include a real Hollywood film, one that's intended to appeal to a
mass commercial audience.

JOE: There must be quite a number of those.

KATIE: Yes, but I've picked the 1996 film of *Hamlet*. It included every line of the text, but   *Q28*
it's more like a typical action hero movie – there are loads of special effects, but no
unifying interpretation of the play.

JOE: All show and no substance.

KATIE: Exactly. Then there's *Prospero's Books*, based on *The Tempest*. That was really   *Q29*
innovative, from a stylistic point of view.

JOE:	Didn't it include dance and singing and animation, as well as live actors?	
KATIE:	Yes, it did. I also want to mention *Looking for Richard*. Did you ever see it?	*Q30*
JOE:	No, but I've read about it. It was a blend of a documentary with a few scenes from *Richard III*, wasn't it?	
KATIE:	That's right. It's more a way of looking into how people nowadays connect with the playwright – the play is really just the starting point. And that'll be where I finish.	
JOE:	Well, it sounds as though it'll be very interesting.	

SECTION 4

This lecture will be about the science of acoustics, the study of sound, in relation to urban environments such as cities. As an acoustic engineer myself, I think this is an area where we're likely to see great changes. In the past, researching urban soundscapes was simple. We measured levels of sound in decibels, so I used to take my sound meter and I measured the noise somewhere, and then I might ask a sample of people to say at what level the sound became annoying.

With data like this, acoustic engineers have been able to build up what we call noise maps, maps of the sound environment. But actually these aren't a lot of use. What they do show is that the highest noise levels are generally on roads – well, that's not really very surprising. But there's quite a lot going on that these maps don't show, because they can't capture the complex way that sound varies over time. So they ignore important issues such as the noise someone might hear from the open windows or gardens of their neighbours, and this *Q31* sort of noise can be quite significant in summer. We don't have any databases on this sort of information. As well as that, these records of sound levels take no account of the fact that people vary in their perceptions of noise – so someone like me with years of working in acoustics might be very different from you in that regard.

But anyway, even though these noise maps are fairly crude, they've been useful in providing *Q32* information and raising awareness that noise matters, we need to deal with it and so it's a political matter. And that's important – we need rules and regulations because noise can cause all sorts of problems.

Those of you who are city-dwellers know that things go on 24 hours a day, so city-dwellers often suffer from interrupted sleep. It's also known that noise can lead to a rise in levels of stress, due to physical changes in the body affecting the composition of the blood. And there are other problems as well, for instance if schoolchildren don't have a quiet place to study, *Q33* their work will suffer.

Now, one problem with decibel measurement is that it doesn't differentiate between different types of noise. Some types of sounds that most people would probably think of as nice and *Q34* relaxing might well score quite highly in decibel levels – think of the sound made by a fountain in a town square, for example. That's not necessarily something that we'd want to control or reduce. So maybe researchers should consider these sorts of sounds in urban design. This is going to be tricky because just measuring decibel levels isn't going to help us here. Instead, *Q35* many researchers are using social science techniques, studying people's emotional response to sound by using questionnaires and so on.

So what exactly do people want to hear in an urban environment? Some recent interdisciplinary research has come out with results that at first sight seem contradictory – a *Q36* city needs to have a sense of activity, so it needs to be lively, with sounds like the clack of high heels on a pavement or the hiss of a coffee machine, but these mustn't be too intrusive, because at the same time we need to be able to relax.

One of the major problems in achieving this will be getting architects and town planners to use the research. Apart from studying the basics of acoustics, these people receive very little training in this area. But in fact they should be regarding sound as an opportunity to add to the experience of urban living, whereas at present they tend to see it as something to be avoided or reduced as far as possible, or something that's just a job for engineers like the street drainage system.

Q37

What's needed is for noise in cities to be regarded as an aesthetic quality, as something that has the qualities of an art form. If we acknowledge this, then we urgently need to know what governs it and how designers can work with it. We need to develop a complex understanding of many factors. What is the relationship between sound and culture? What can we learn from disciplines such as psychology about the way that sound interacts with human development and social relationships, and the way that sound affects our thought and feelings? Can we learn anything from physics about the nature of sound itself?

Q38

Q39

Today's powerful technologies can also help us. To show us their ideas and help us to imagine the effect their buildings will have, architects and town planners already use virtual reality – but these programs are silent. In the future such programs could use realistic sounds, meaning that soundscapes could be explored before being built. So hopefully, using the best technology we can lay our hands on, the city of the future will be a pleasure to the ears as well as the eyes.

Q40

Listening and Reading Answer Keys

TEST 5

LISTENING

Section 1, Questions 1–10

1 mountains
2 horse
3 garden(s)
4 lunch
5 map
6 experience
7 Ratchesons
8 helmet
9 shops
10 267

Section 2, Questions 11–20

11 A
12 A
13 C
14 C
15&16 *IN EITHER ORDER*
    A
    E
17 F
18 C
19 D
20 B

Section 3, Questions 21–30

21 B
22 C
23 C
24 budget
25 employment
26 safety
27 insurance
28 diary
29 database
30 museum

Section 4, Questions 31–40

31 damage
32 side effects
33 bridge
34 confusion
35 smartphone
36 resources
37 unnecessary/not necessary
38 chocolate bar
39 problem
40 market share

If you score …

0–15	16–24	25–40
you are unlikely to get an acceptable score under examination conditions and we recommend that you spend a lot of time improving your English before you take IELTS.	you may get an acceptable score under examination conditions but we recommend that you think about having more practice or lessons before you take IELTS.	you are likely to get an acceptable score under examination conditions but remember that different institutions will find different scores acceptable.

READING

Reading Passage 1, Questions 1–13

1 NOT GIVEN
2 FALSE
3 FALSE
4 TRUE
5 TRUE
6 taste
7 cheaper
8 convenient
9 image
10 sustainable
11 recycled
12 biodiversity
13 desertification

Reading Passage 2, Questions 14–26

14 antiques
15 triumph
16 information
17 contact/meetings
18 hunt/desire
19 aimless/empty
20 educational
21 Trainspotting
22 NOT GIVEN
23 FALSE
24 NOT GIVEN
25 TRUE
26 TRUE

Reading Passage 3, Questions 27–40

27 vi
28 viii
29 ii
30 iv
31 iii
32 vii
33 fire science
34 investigators
35 evidence
36 prosecution
37 NOT GIVEN
38 YES
39 NO
40 NO

If you score ...

0–15	16–25	26–40
you are unlikely to get an acceptable score under examination conditions and we recommend that you spend a lot of time improving your English before you take IELTS.	you may get an acceptable score under examination conditions but we recommend that you think about having more practice or lessons before you take IELTS.	you are likely to get an acceptable score under examination conditions but remember that different institutions will find different scores acceptable.

TEST 6

LISTENING

Section 1, Questions 1–10

1	2.45
2	band
3	play
4	scientist
5	river
6	grandparents
7	Handsworth
8	traditional
9	outdoor
10	logo

Section 2, Questions 11–20

11	B
12	C
13	A
14	B
15	C
16	F
17	B
18	E
19	G
20	C

Section 3, Questions 21–30

21	C
22	B
23	C
24	A
25	C
26	E
27	G
28	D
29	C
30	A

Section 4, Questions 31–40

31	bullying
32	superiority
33	personality
34	structural
35	absence
36	confidence
37	visions
38	democratic
39	respect
40	mediator

If you score …

0–16	17–25	26–40
you are unlikely to get an acceptable score under examination conditions and we recommend that you spend a lot of time improving your English before you take IELTS.	you may get an acceptable score under examination conditions but we recommend that you think about having more practice or lessons before you take IELTS.	you are likely to get an acceptable score under examination conditions but remember that different institutions will find different scores acceptable.

READING

Reading Passage 1, Questions 1–13

1	A
2	B
3	H
4	D
5	B
6	C
7	G
8	B
9	A

10&11 *IN EITHER ORDER*
    D
    E

12&13 *IN EITHER ORDER*
    C
    D

Reading Passage 2, Questions 14–26

14	iv
15	vi
16	viii
17	v
18	i
19	vii
20	iii
21	TRUE
22	FALSE
23	FALSE
24	NOT GIVEN
25	rubber
26	farmer

Reading Passage 3, Questions 27–40

27	eye movements
28	language co-activation
29	Stroop Task
30	conflict management
31	cognitive control
32	YES
33	NOT GIVEN
34	NO
35	NO
36	NOT GIVEN
37	D
38	G
39	B
40	C

If you score …

0–15	16–25	26–40
you are unlikely to get an acceptable score under examination conditions and we recommend that you spend a lot of time improving your English before you take IELTS.	you may get an acceptable score under examination conditions but we recommend that you think about having more practice or lessons before you take IELTS.	you are likely to get an acceptable score under examination conditions but remember that different institutions will find different scores acceptable.

TEST 7

LISTENING

Section 1, Questions 1–10

1 travel/travel(l)ing
2 history
3 study
4 teenagers
5 kitchen
6 crime
7 appointment/booking
8 sugar
9 stamps
10 parking

Section 2, Questions 11–20

11&12 IN EITHER ORDER
    D
    E
13&14 IN EITHER ORDER
    A
    C
15 C
16 B
17 A
18 stress
19 weight
20 families

Section 3, Questions 21–30

21 C
22 E
23 H
24 B
25 A
26 F
27 A
28 C
29 B
30 B

Section 4, Questions 31–40

31 insects
32 behaviour/behavior
33 father
34 complex/complicated
35 reproduction/breeding
36 control
37 duck(s)
38 language
39 food
40 cost(s)/price(s)/bill(s)

If you score …

0–15	16–25	26–40
you are unlikely to get an acceptable score under examination conditions and we recommend that you spend a lot of time improving your English before you take IELTS.	you may get an acceptable score under examination conditions but we recommend that you think about having more practice or lessons before you take IELTS.	you are likely to get an acceptable score under examination conditions but remember that different institutions will find different scores acceptable.

READING

Reading Passage 1, Questions 1–13

1 v
2 iii
3 viii
4 i
5 iv
6 vi
7 ii
8 pirates
9 food
10 oil
11 settlers
12 species
13 eggs

Reading Passage 2, Questions 14–26

14 D
15 C
16 F
17 G
18 D
19 B
20 vaccinations
21 antibiotics
22 mosquito(e)s
23 factories
24 forests
25 Polio
26 mountain

Reading Passage 3, Questions 27–40

27 dopamine
28 pleasure
29 caudate
30 anticipatory phase
31 food
32 B
33 C
34 A
35 B
36 D
37 F
38 B
39 E
40 C

If you score …

0–14	15–24	25–40
you are unlikely to get an acceptable score under examination conditions and we recommend that you spend a lot of time improving your English before you take IELTS.	you may get an acceptable score under examination conditions but we recommend that you think about having more practice or lessons before you take IELTS.	you are likely to get an acceptable score under examination conditions but remember that different institutions will find different scores acceptable.

TEST 8

LISTENING

Section 1, Questions 1–10

1	temporary
2	doctor
3	Africa
4	youth
5	May
6	cheese
7	Arbuthnot
8	DG7 4PH
9	Tuesday
10	talk/presentation

Section 2, Questions 11–20

11	A
12	C
13	B
14	B
15	H
16	C
17	F
18	G
19	I
20	B

Section 3, Questions 21–30

21	classification
22	worst
23	slides
24	issues
25	F
26	A
27	E
28	C
29	G
30	B

Section 4, Questions 31–40

31	garden(s)
32	political
33	work/study
34	fountain
35	social
36	lively
37	training
38	culture
39	nature
40	silent

If you score …

0–15	16–24	25–40
you are unlikely to get an acceptable score under examination conditions and we recommend that you spend a lot of time improving your English before you take IELTS.	you may get an acceptable score under examination conditions but we recommend that you think about having more practice or lessons before you take IELTS.	you are likely to get an acceptable score under examination conditions but remember that different institutions will find different scores acceptable.

READING

Reading Passage 1,
Questions 1–13

1	obsidian
2	spears
3	beads
4	impurities
5	Romans
6	lead
7	clouding
8	taxes
9	TRUE
10	FALSE
11	NOT GIVEN
12	TRUE
13	FALSE

Reading Passage 2,
Questions 14–26

14	D
15	A
16	C
17	A
18	C
19	E
20	D
21	F
22	A
23	NO
24	NOT GIVEN
25	YES
26	YES

Reading Passage 3,
Questions 27–40

27	iv
28	ii
29	vi
30	viii
31	vii
32	i
33	iii
34	YES
35	NOT GIVEN
36	NO
37	NO
38	information
39	financial
40	shareholders/investors

If you score …

0–14	15–24	25–40
you are unlikely to get an acceptable score under examination conditions and we recommend that you spend a lot of time improving your English before you take IELTS.	you may get an acceptable score under examination conditions but we recommend that you think about having more practice or lessons before you take IELTS.	you are likely to get an acceptable score under examination conditions but remember that different institutions will find different scores acceptable.

Sample answers for Writing tasks

TEST 5, WRITING TASK 1

SAMPLE ANSWER

This is an answer written by a candidate who achieved a **Band 5.0** score. Here is the examiner's comment:

> The candidate covers the key features and rounds off the description with an overview. Organisation is evident, however not wholly logical, and it is sometimes difficult to relate data to specific age groups. Vocabulary is just about adequate, but is rather dependent on input material [*regular physical activity | percentage*]: original material is limited to e.g. [*teenager | mid-twenties*] with a lot of inaccuracy in word formation. Most sentence forms consist of simple structures and these are often inaccurate [*bars's changed and interesting | men's percentage are increasing | the percentage more decrease until*], though there is some accuracy in comparative forms [*is higher than*].

The bar chart below shows the percentage of Australia men and women in different age group who did regular physical activity in 2010. It's interesting to the bar chart.

In 15 to 24, , Australian men's percentage of doing regular physical activity is 52.8 and women's percentage is 47.7. Compare with men and women, men's percentage is higher than women's percentage. However, bars's changed and interesting. After 25 to 64, men's percentage are increasing. In 25 to 34, men's percentage is 42,2. Besides, In 35 to 44, the percentage more decrease until 39.5.

After over 45 age, a few increase like 43.7, 45.1 and 46.7.

However, the percentage couldn't over 50%.

Then, women's percentages are increase until 54 age like 52.5, 53.3. Although women's percentages are decrease after 55 age, the percentages are higher than men's percentages.

In conclusion, men did regular physical activity more than women when they were teenager and mid twenties.

After mid-twenties, however, men's percentage was decreased and women's percentage was increase.

TEST 5, WRITING TASK 2

SAMPLE ANSWER

This is an answer written by a candidate who achieved a **Band 6.0** score. Here is the examiner's comment:

> The candidate addresses all parts of the prompt, although there is some misunderstanding of the term ***shared freely***. Ideas relating to each sector mentioned in the prompt are presented, yet there is not much development of these, especially of sharing ideas in the business world. There is a clear overall progression, with the candidate's own opinion presented at the end, but there are some errors in the use of cohesive devices [*working there on out of this | which scientist*]. Lexis is mainly appropriate for the task, though there are some errors in word choice [*actual | releases*] and spelling [*govenment | limite | theme | loose*]. There is a mix of simple and complex sentence forms, with a fair degree of accuracy: errors in grammatical control seldom prevent meaning from coming through.

Sharing information is actual issue in our world where it has strong influence on people. There are various spheres of our life where information is more or less important for people working there on out of this. For this reason some people consider that it is good to share information while others think in opposite way.

For example, practically all scientists are glad to share information with ordinary people or other scientist. There is no competition in this sphere. Sometimes it is bad for govenment which scientist share the secret information with international spy but it will not hurt information.

There are some simple rules in academic world which limite informational sources between people. If person is interested in theme discussing with you and you are ready to keep talking then the person gives you all information what he knows for free. On the other hand, if the person knows much and he knows that you can not give him actual or new information then he will share information with you just for money. For example, student pay for his learning while two students can cooperate and share information with each other. It is obviously that sharing information in business world can followes by releases. There is large competition and it may takes much costs for companies. Companies loose their profit every day because some one can not keep silence especially IT companies.

To sum up all above it is neccessery to say that there are some spheres in which sharing information is a crime. In my opinion, in many cases information can be too important or sharing at all.

TEST 6, WRITING TASK 1

SAMPLE ANSWER

This is an answer written by a candidate who achieved a **Band 7.0** score. Here is the examiner's comment:

> The candidate covers all the key features and presents a clear overview of the developments planned. Information and ideas are logically organised and there is a clear progression throughout the response. A range of cohesive devices is used flexibly [*currently* | *Overall* | *First of all* | *therefore* | *Moreover* | *The next point* | *To sum up*]. Lexical choice shows flexibility and precision, and includes less common items [*modifications* | *predicting* | *grouped in a shopping mall*], though there is some inappropriate word choice [*deserves*]. A range of grammatical structures is used flexibly and accurately and error-free sentences are frequent.

The two maps of the centre of the towns of Islip give information about the city currently and in the future. Overall, a lot of modifications can be observed during the forecast development.

First of all, according to the current map the centre is close to a countryside. A main road deserves houses, a school, several shops and a park.

Looking more closely at the map predicting the future development of the city, a lot of modifications can be observed. The size of the centre will increase in an oval shape; therefore the countryside will disappear. Moreover, the single road will be replaced by a bigger dual carriageway. A pedestrian way will deserve the central area. New houses will be built with new facilities such as a bus station and a parking. The shops will be grouped in a shopping mall. The next point is the garden area which will be smaller. As the city will have more people the school will be bigger.

To sum up, between the actual map of Islip town centre and the future planned development, a lot of modifications are predicted. On the one hand the city will be bigger with more facilities. On the other hand the park will be reduced and the countryside will disappear. The city will have changed a great deal.

TEST 6, WRITING TASK 2

SAMPLE ANSWER

This is an answer written by a candidate who achieved a **Band 5.0** score. Here is the examiner's comment:

> The response looks at some advantages and disadvantages of the topic, but does not reach any conclusion. As a result, there is a lack of overall progression, although organisation is evident and cohesive devices are used (though rather mechanically) [*One of advantages | For example | Also | Another disadvantage | For instance*]. The range of lexis is adequate for the task, however there are often spelling mistakes [*contries | yonge | quilified*] and errors in word choice or formation [*chancing to improve | unemployee problem*]. There are attempts to produce complex sentence forms, but there is a lack of grammatical control which can cause some difficulty for the reader [*… due to some countries limit the population, if that have more young children it will over limit*].

Nowadays, the people of some countries that have the young people more than the old people. Some people thinks when their contries have the yonge people more than the old people will be good because, that could increases the population in the future. Another people thinks it not good due to some countries limit the population, if that have more young children, it will over limit. This essay will discuss the advantages and disadvantages about in some countries have the young people more than the old people.

One of advantages is increasing the population. In some countries support the family to have more children because that can increases the population in the future. For example, in Singapore, Philiphine and so on. What is more chancing to improve the educations as when they have a lot of young generation, the government could improve a good education. Also, they can develop the systems include the quilified teachers, the good atmosphere.

One of disadvantages is the place for study. If the young generation still a lot, the school will not enough for the study, the government should construct more school. Also, when they have the new schools, the teacher will not enough to teach them. The university should get more student to study about teaching education.

Another disadvantages is the quality of education. If the many students learn in the classroom, the teachers can not take care all. For instance, when they have a problem they will need some help from the teachers. Furthermore, when they grow up, the unemployee problem will happen because the company can not receive everybody to get a job.

In conclusion, in some countries that have the young population more than the old population, the government should manage the education system. Moreover, they should prepare the plans for sloving unemployee problems which can happen in the future.

TEST 7, WRITING TASK 1

SAMPLE ANSWER

This is an answer written by a candidate who achieved a **Band 6.5** score. Here is the examiner's comment:

> The candidate organises the information well and describes the trends in the various groups, but the lack of data to support the descriptions is a significant omission. There is a clear progression throughout the response, with good management of cohesive devices [*percentage of people who | during the same period | in these segments of the chart | the groups in which | such facilities*]. Lexis shows some flexibility and precision [*on a weekly basis*] and there is evidence of less common items [*segments | major changes | most of the population | most/least popular | with the exception of*], with few errors in word choice [*visualises | be | clients*]. There is a variety of complex structures used with flexibility and accuracy, but there are also a few errors in grammatical control and in punctuation.

The chart visualises how often the US citizens be at fast-food restaurants in the years 2003, 2006 and 2013.

From 2003 to 2006 the percentage of people who have never eaten at a fast food restaurant has fallen by 1%, but on the other hand during the same period the number of clients who eat fast food everyday has also fallen to about 3% of the population. Since 2006, no other changes have occurred in these segments of the chart.

The major changes can be seen in the groups, who eat in a fast-food restaurant on a weekly basis (once or several times a week) and in the groups in which people visit the fast-food restaurants once or twice a month or once a few months. While in 2006 most of the US citizens ate at such facilities at least once a week, in 2013 most of the population did so only once or twice a month. It's clear that the fast-food restaurants were most popular in 2006 and least popular in 2013. However the number of people who eat in such restaurants only a few times every year didn't change.

As a whole, with the exception of people who rarely or never eat fast food and in addition, the small part of the population who eat every day, the peak of going to fast-food restaurants was reached in 2006 in contrast with 2013 when most of the population spent time in them only once or twice a month.

TEST 7, WRITING TASK 2

SAMPLE ANSWER

This is an answer written by a candidate who achieved a **Band 7.5** score. Here is the examiner's comment:

> This is a good response which would achieve an even higher score if there was more focus on **large sums of money** and on **between cities**. The writing is well organised and there is a clear progression throughout, although the use of some cohesive devices could be more flexible. There is a wide range of vocabulary, used appropriately and naturally, [*preferred method of transportation | leave the driving to the professional | more affordable | ever-expanding urban populations | embrace the idea of*], but some spelling errors are noted [*Communters | whill | cheif | ammount | busses*]. There is a wide range of structures and again, these are used flexibly, however there are occasional errors in punctuation.

For many people around the world, the preferred method of transportation is high-speed rail. Communters travelling to and from work rely on the safety and efficiency, whill tourists appreciate the convenience and novelty that trains provide. Others believe that highways, busses and regular trains should be improved before new, high-speed lines are added.

Safety is cheif among concerns for those who travel to work or school on a regular basis. If one drives a car, they have to concentrate on the road not only to avoid accidents but also to prevent other drivers from causing a problem on the road. High-speed rail allows the communter to leave the driving to the professional controlling the train, allowing them to get some work done while getting to work safely.

In addition, people tend to move further and further away from city centres, where land and houses are more affordable. High-speed rail allows these commuters to travel greater distances in a shorter ammount of time. There is a flow-on effect here, because if we can reduce the number of cars on the road, we can also cut down on traffic jams and road delays.

On the other hand, high-speed trains are expensive, and some believe this money could be spend on repairing motorways which are used by cars, busses and motorcycles. Another possibility would be to use this money to build more regular communter trains and busses to service the ever-expanding urban populations. Moreover, boats and ferries could benefit from a budget which focuses more on existing forms of transport.

In the end, public transport is an issue which affects us all. The taxes which we pay should be spent on the type of transport which will have the most benefit to all citizens. In addition, we need to take into account how much the environment is damaged by fossil fuels and pollution. therefore, I believe in order to move forward, we need to embrace the idea of high-speed rail so that future generations can continue to live safely and efficiently.

TEST 8, WRITING TASK 1

SAMPLE ANSWER

This is an answer written by a candidate who achieved a **Band 6.0** score. Here is the examiner's comment:

> The candidate has provided a clear introduction and an overview of the key stages of the process. Each stage is identified and described, although there are some minor errors in the reporting of stage 5. There is room for expansion of the description of each stage, which could help to achieve a higher score. There is a clear overall progression, with each stage being signalled by appropriate markers [*First* | *in order to* | *After that* | *At this point* | *Then, the final step* | *Finally*]. These markers are adequate, but a higher score might be achieved by varying their position in each sentence, rather than always placing them at the beginning. The range of vocabulary is adequate for the task and there are attempts to use more variety here [*five general steps* | *connected* | *accumulated*], though there are some examples of error in word choice [*box* / tank | *a circle movements* / a circular movement], in spelling [*undergrownd* | *trough* | *conteiner* | *sumary*] and in word formation [*condensered* / condensed | *gas* / gaseous | *trasladated* / transferred? | *condensering* / condensing]. There is a mix of simple and complex sentence forms, including accurate use of passive forms. There are some errors [*a* / *an* | *who* / *what*], but otherwise the level of accuracy is good. The same level of accuracy, over a wider range of sentence forms, would increase the score on Grammatical Range and Accuracy.

The diagram shows how electricity is produced by geothermal energy. There are five general steps in this process. First, in a big box connected underground, cold water is accumulated in order to be pumped down about 4.5 Km.

After that, water is heated passing trough hot rocks called Geothermal zone and it is pumped up in order to be condensered in a big conteiner. At this point, water is in a gas state and it is put in a turbine which moves it in a circle movements. Then, the final step is to use a generator in order to water be powered and energy can be produced. Finally energy is trasladated to a energy tower.

In sumary, the geothermal power plant is used to create energy in some steps: heating cold water by a geothermal zone and condensering it in order to put it in a generator turbine which is who produces the energy to be used.

TEST 8, WRITING TASK 2

SAMPLE ANSWER

This is an answer written by a candidate who achieved a **Band 5.0** score. Here is the examiner's comment:

> This is an attempt to address the prompt and some main ideas are put forward, but there is no discussion of *is likely to result in a society of individuals who only think about their own wishes*. This omission, and the fact that the response is underlength, limit the Band score rating. Organisation is evident, however the answer lacks contextualisation, and cohesion within sentences is sometimes faulty [*that is cause many African children to … | they will show respect to their ad community in is general*]. Vocabulary is the strongest aspect of the response [*confident | make mistakes | dictate | the right path | do something wrong | manage their affairs | vandals and aggressors | determine their own choices | show respect | oppressed | respect children | justify*] and although spelling errors occur, they do not generally prevent meaning from coming through [*becouse | tought | smagging*]. Grammatical control is variable: some complex structures are produced accurately while other, simpler, forms contain errors. Punctuation and capitalisation are also sometimes faulty.

it is good to show children living a freedom evironment, becouse it could help children to grow stronger and confident. But it depends on the age of the child, forexample a little children can not choose clothes and they also like to eat sweets all the time.

When the children is free to their choices they could make mistakes so parents should not dictate children what want, but guide to the right path. forexample most parents in western world teach their children arguing rather than smagging when they do something wrong. When children are tought to do their own choice could easily manage their affairs, when grow up.

children may sometimes give a good opinion, so that it is good to understand rather than upsetting them. Many parents In Africa do not believe of listen children, that is cause many African children become vandals and aggressors toward the community.

if we teach our youngers to determine their own choices, they will show respect to their ad community in is general because they never felt oppressed and they would not bother to any when they get older.

over all, when we listen our children that we make their future personality better. parents should respect children. Same like adults. When the parents try to refuse children something they should justify to them why they refused explain to them the reasons.

Sample answer sheets

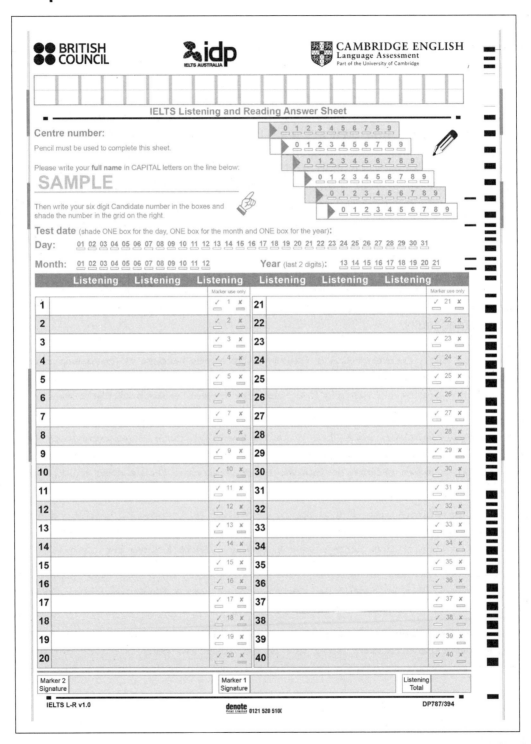

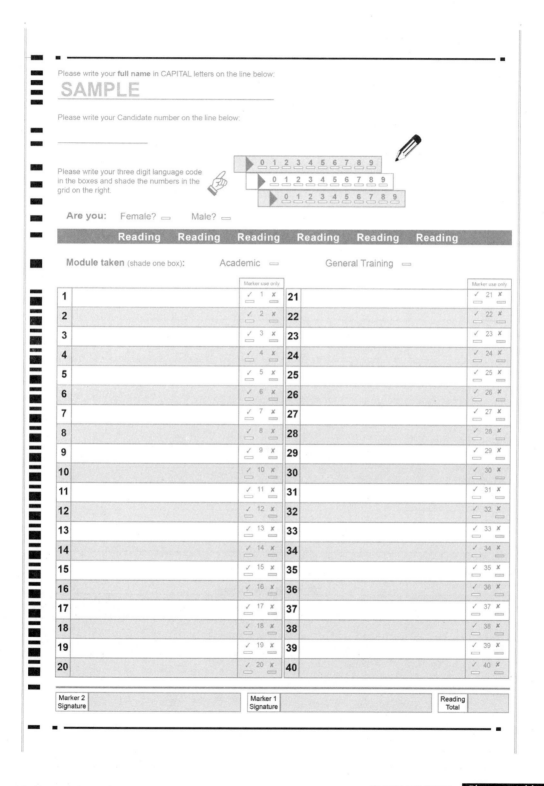

Please write your **full name** in CAPITAL letters on the line below:

SAMPLE

Please write your Candidate number on the line below:

Please write your three digit language code in the boxes and shade the numbers in the grid on the right.

0 1 2 3 4 5 6 7 8 9
0 1 2 3 4 5 6 7 8 9
0 1 2 3 4 5 6 7 8 9

Are you: Female? ⎕ Male? ⎕

Reading Reading Reading Reading Reading Reading

Module taken (shade one box): Academic ⎕ General Training ⎕

	Marker use only			Marker use only
1	✓ 1 ✗	21		✓ 21 ✗
2	✓ 2 ✗	22		✓ 22 ✗
3	✓ 3 ✗	23		✓ 23 ✗
4	✓ 4 ✗	24		✓ 24 ✗
5	✓ 5 ✗	25		✓ 25 ✗
6	✓ 6 ✗	26		✓ 26 ✗
7	✓ 7 ✗	27		✓ 27 ✗
8	✓ 8 ✗	28		✓ 28 ✗
9	✓ 9 ✗	29		✓ 29 ✗
10	✓ 10 ✗	30		✓ 30 ✗
11	✓ 11 ✗	31		✓ 31 ✗
12	✓ 12 ✗	32		✓ 32 ✗
13	✓ 13 ✗	33		✓ 33 ✗
14	✓ 14 ✗	34		✓ 34 ✗
15	✓ 15 ✗	35		✓ 35 ✗
16	✓ 16 ✗	36		✓ 36 ✗
17	✓ 17 ✗	37		✓ 37 ✗
18	✓ 18 ✗	38		✓ 38 ✗
19	✓ 19 ✗	39		✓ 39 ✗
20	✓ 20 ✗	40		✓ 40 ✗

Marker 2 Signature		Marker 1 Signature		Reading Total	

●● BRITISH
●● COUNCIL   **idp** IELTS AUSTRALIA   **CAMBRIDGE ENGLISH**
Language Assessment
Part of the University of Cambridge

IELTS Writing Answer Sheet – TASK 1

Candidate Name

Centre Number

Candidate Number

Module (shade one box):   Academic ▭   General Training ▭

Test date

D D   M M   Y Y Y Y

TASK 1

Do not write below this line

100913/2

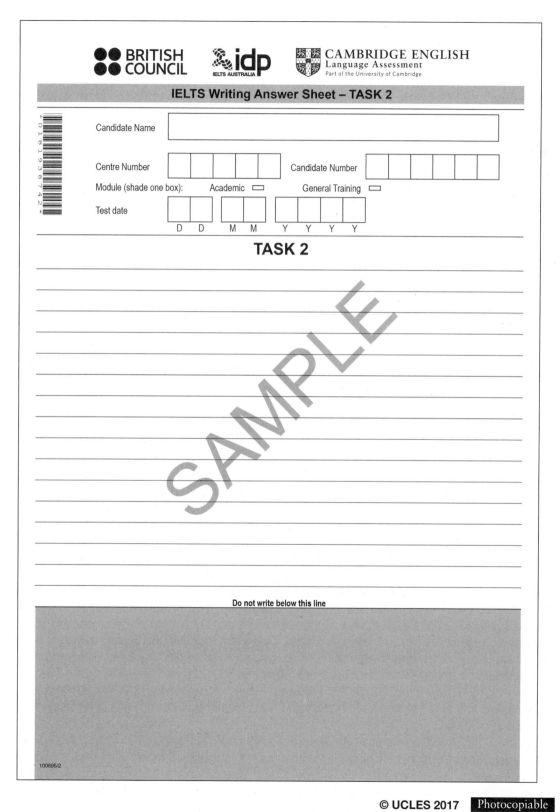

IELTS Writing Answer Sheet – TASK 2

Candidate Name

Centre Number

Candidate Number

Module (shade one box): Academic ☐ General Training ☐

Test date

D D M M Y Y Y Y

TASK 2

Do not write below this line

Acknowledgements

The authors and publishers acknowledge the following sources of copyright material and are grateful for the permissions granted. While every effort has been made, it has not always been possible to identify the sources of all the material used, or to trace all copyright holders. If any omissions are brought to our notice, we will be happy to include the appropriate acknowledgements on reprinting and in the next update to the digital edition, as applicable.

Text on pp. 16–17 adapted from 'Staying Power' by Martin Symington. Copyright © 2013 *Geographical Magazine*. Reproduced with permission; Text on pp. 24–25 adapted from 'Moral Moments: Unprincipled Principles' by Joel Marks. Copyright © 2006 Joel Marks. Reproduced with kind permission; Graph on p. 27 adapted from 'Participation in Exercise, Recreation and Sport Survey 2010 Annual Report'. Copyright © Standing Committee on Recreation and Sport 2. Reproduced with permission of Australian Sports Commission; Text on pp. 36–38 adapted from 'The Future of Agriculture: Synthesis of an online debate' by Maya Manzi and Gine Zwart. Copyright © 2013 Oxfam. Reproduced with the permission of Oxfam, Oxfam House, John Smith Drive, Cowley, Oxford OX4 2JY, UK www.oxfam.org.uk; Text on pp. 43–44 adapted from 'Finding the lost city' by Hugh Thomson. Copyright © 2011 *Geographical Magazine*. Reproduced with permission; Text on pp. 46–47 adapted from 'The Cognitive Benefits of Being Bilingual' by Viorica Marian and Anthony Shook. Copyright © 2012 Cerebrum- The Dana Foundation. Reproduced with kind permission of The Dana Foundation; Text on pp. 60–61 adapted from 'Flying Tortoises' by Mauricio Handler. Copyright © 2012 *Geographical Magazine*. Reproduced with permission; Text on pp. 63–64 adapted from 'The Intersection of Health Sciences and Geography' by Elizabeth Borneman. Copyright © 2014 Geo Lounge. Reproduced with kind permission; Text on pp. 66–67 adapted from 'The Neuroscience of Music' by Jonah Lehrer, *Wired Magazine* 2012. Copyright © 2011 Condé Nast. Reproduced with permission. Chart on p. 71 adapted from '1 in 5 Americans Eat Fast Food Several Times a Week' by Niall McCarthy. Copyright © 2013 Statista, Inc. Reproduced with kind permission; Text on pp. 80–81 adapted from 'History of Glass'. Copyright © British Glass. Reproduced with kind permission; Text on pp. 83–84 adapted from 'Bring back the big cats: is it time to start rewilding Britain?' by George Monbiot. Copyright © 2014 New Statesman Limited. Reproduced with permission; Text on pp. 89–90 adapted from 'It's time for better boards' by Denise Kingsmill. Copyright © 2013 Management Today. Reproduced with permission of Haymarket Media Group Ltd; Text on p. 92 adapted from 'Geothermal Power Plants'; Text on pp. 95–96 adapted from 'Walter Peak Guided Cycling'. Copyright © Real Journeys 2017. Reproduced with kind permission; Text on pp. 98–99 adapted from 'Sacred Cow or Trojan Horse?' by Ben Walker. Copyright © 2015 CMI's Insights web channel at managers.org.uk/insights. Reproduced with kind permission of Chartered Management Institute; Text on pp. 104–105 adapted from 'Fight the good fight- Professional Manager, Summer 2013'. Copyright © 2013 CMI's Insights web channel at managers.org.uk/insights. Reproduced with kind permission of Chartered Management Institute; Text on pp. 106–107 adapted from 'The Consumer Holiday Trends Report ABTA Consumer Survey 2013'. Copyright © ABTA Ltd. Reproduced with kind permission; Text on pp. 106–107 adapted from 'About our Fitness Holidays'. Copyright © Health and Fitness Travel Ltd. Reproduced with kind permission; Text on pp. 109–110 adapted from 'Mercury hurts birds and people: what we can learn from studying our feathered friends' by Jenny R. Isaacs, interview by Claire Varian-Ramos. Copyright © Mongabay. Reproduced with permission.